Praise for *The Man Yo*

A great book for men that women will wa
is genuine, gracious, gifted, and a gentlem
with wisdom and wit.
CANON J. JOHN, director, Philo Trust

Anthony Delaney is one of God's chosen vessels. He is surely one of tomorrow's
men!
R. T. KENDALL, president, R.T. Kendall Ministries

Get this book. It's not full of theories—it's down to earth, practical, and deals
with the kind of issues we all need help with.
ERIC DELVE, Art of Leadership company

Tackles head-on what we need to become the men we ought to be. *The Man
You Were Made to Be* nails it!
CARL BEECH, CVM, Elim, founder of Codelife movement

Anthony Delaney is a rare breed of male leader. Not only does he practice what
he preaches, but the combination of strength and genuine humility, compassion,
and determination (as well as a down to earth sense of humour!) makes him
superbly qualified to speak into the lives of other men.
LUCY PEPPIATT, principal, Westminster Theological Centre

Anthony is a rare kind of man—a great leader, honest about his weaknesses,
charismatic but surprisingly self-effacing. He comes from an ordinary background but has never settled for mediocrity. A strong man, with a tender heart.
This excellent book speaks to every man who lives with the tests, conflicts,
hopes, and desires that crowd our daily lives, combining fresh insights with
ancient truths to find a new way to express authentic masculinity.
MIKE BREEN, 3DM Global Team Leader

In my line of work I'm busy assessing the true value of beautiful diamonds. How
much more valuable is a man's life! This book is written by a good friend who
is utterly focused on reflecting the Lord in his own life. Within these pages he
unlocks some deep and lasting treasures for any man looking to become more
who he was made to be.
JODY WAINWRIGHT, director, Boodles (subject of TV documentary *The
Million Pound Necklace*)

In no-nonsense, power-packed language, Anthony Delaney shows how any
old lump of coal can become a diamond—brilliant!
PROFESSOR LEONARD SWEET, futurist and bestselling author

Anthony Delaney is one of those amazing leaders who is truly authentic in his faith, impacting his community and building a network of reproducing churches. I'm truly inspired by his get-it-done attitude while totally depending on God.

DAVE FERGUSON, director of NewThing and president of Exponential

Communicates in a way that is grounded in honesty, reality, and integrity. Smashes every religious stereotype you've ever come across.

PROFESSOR PAUL MCGEE, ("the SUMO guy"), bestselling author and business coach

A must for any man who aspires to make a difference. Anthony speaks powerfully from and to the heart, but in his own life he acts on these messages which makes him the best friend a guy could ask for!

JOHN ANON, CEO, Safe And Free (international anti-trafficking charity)

I had the privilege of working very closely with the author in what in those days was nothing less than a war zone. As a tough cop he was no stranger to the violent and corrupt underbelly of Manchester's inner city. If you find yourself keeping God at arm's length because of all that macho stuff, this book will change your life.

TONY FITZGERALD, Urban Legend

Anthony is a rare man . . . one of a kind. He's powerful with deep purpose, who uses this to help others. I think he does it because he genuinely cares and is kind enough to bother. He is just the sort of man that we need more of in our communities. Why should you read this book? Because Anthony's passion shows through in every page, and the wisdom he offers will challenge and help you. Be bold . . . read on!

JAMES RAY, CEO of Xtreme Character Challenge Adventure

I have benefited multiple times from Anthony's wisdom and wide-ranging experience. This book reflects this accumulated learning and wisdom on critically important issues with which most, if not all, men wrestle. He addresses the issues with wit and honesty, based on personal experience and biblical teaching. It is my hope that men will read and reflect on this book—especially those who want nothing to do with church, God, or Jesus.

GARY SCHWAMMLEIN, President Emeritus, Global Leadership Network

The bins need taking out.

ZOE DELANEY

ANTHONY DELANEY FRSA **(Fellow of the Royal Society) is married to Zoe, father of three, and grandfather of six at the last count.** He served for over ten years in Greater Manchester Police, including time on the riot squad and plain clothes vice units. He left the police service following a call to lead churches. Thirteen years ago, he returned to Manchester to lead Ivy Church, which has become a church planting network—the growth of which has been featured in national press including a six page article in *The Independent*.

He is a faculty member of Westminster Theological Centre accredited by the University of Chester lecturing on Leadership. Having spoken at national and international conferences such as New Wine, Spring Harvest, Viral (Kenya), Exponential USA, and the Global Leadership Summit. He founded the LAUNCH leadership catalyst to bring leaders from all over the world together for inspiration, imagination, and innovation.

He leads the Western Europe arm of the "New Thing" global network, and his teaching is broadcast regularly from the UK around the world on various radio and TV platforms. His previous book *The B.E.S.T. Marriage: Why Settle For Less?* is also published by Moody/Northfield and Dr. Gary Chapman—author of *The 5 Love Languages*—says it "points the way to a better marriage."

In 2020, Anthony was honored by being made a member of the Royal Society of Arts, an award recognizing the contributions of exceptional individuals from across the world who have made significant contributions to social change.

He blogs at www.anthonydelaney.com.

THE
MAN
YOU
WERE
MADE
TO BE

NOTHING TO PROVE

NOTHING TO HIDE

EVERYTHING TO LIVE FOR

ANTHONY
DELANEY

MOODY PUBLISHERS
CHICAGO

Originally delivered by fleets of horse-drawn wagons, the affordable paperbacks from D. L. Moody's publishing house resourced the church and served everyday people. Now, after more than 125 years of publishing and ministry, Moody Publishers' mission remains the same—even if our delivery systems have changed a bit. For more information on other books (and resources) created from a biblical perspective, go to www.moodypublishers.com or write to:

Moody Publishers
820 N. LaSalle Boulevard
Chicago, IL 60610

1 3 5 7 9 10 8 6 4 2

Printed in the United States of America

*I dedicate this book to the most precious gifts of God in my life:
my loving wife, Zoe; my wonderful children,
Emma, Hannah, and Joel; and to my six grandchildren.
I have learned so much from you all about what really matters
and want to thank you for encouraging me every day.*

*I would also like to thank the Ivy Church family
as we work together to help people find their way back to God, and
Duane and the staff at Moody for all your encouragement
and help to make this "the book it was meant to be."*

Contents

For we are God's masterpiece. He has created us anew in Christ Jesus, so we can do the good things he planned for us long ago.

Ephesians 2:10 (NLT)

Foreword

JESUS WAS UNDOUBTEDLY a man's man—His closest friends were working-class guys with whom He ate, partied, and shared His life, as well as a message of sacrifice, power, and—ultimately—amazing joy. Surely men have got to appreciate that, yet for decades in many nations men have been voting with their feet and leaving the church in droves.

This book is a massive breath of fresh air. Receive wisdom from a truly sharp guy who grew up on Manchester's mean streets before spending several years pounding the beat on some of Europe's most deprived estates. Anthony has witnessed some of the worst life has to offer but became convinced that there is good news relevant to men, even in the most desperate situations.

His faith was proved not just in oak-panelled libraries or lecture rooms but where it counts—on the front line. That's where this book was forged, its earthy wisdom, practical application, and great stories. It's just what real men need in today's confused world.

We have been close for years and he really is a sickeningly great dad, husband, friend, and leader heading up a fast-growing network of churches that (for a change) men want to fully be part of.

You will find *The Man You Were Made to Be* funny, challenging, and life-affirming and it would be my hope that through it, like Anthony and me, you might also discover and meet the ultimate man's man.

ANDY HAWTHORNE (OBE)
Founder and Director, *Message Trust*

A Nation's Strength

What makes a nation's pillars high
And its foundations strong?
What makes it mighty to defy
The foes that round it throng?

It is not gold. Its kingdoms grand
Go down in battle shock;
Its shafts are laid on sinking sand,
Not on abiding rock.

Is it the sword? Ask the red dust
Of empires passed away;
The blood has turned their stones to rust,
Their glory to decay.

And is it pride? Ah, that bright crown
Has seemed to nations sweet;
But God has struck its luster down
In ashes at his feet.

Not gold but only men can make
A people great and strong;
Men who for truth and honor's sake
Stand fast and suffer long.

Brave men who work while others sleep,
Who dare while others fly . . .
They build a nation's pillars deep
And lift them to the sky.

– RALPH WALDO EMERSON

Chapter 1

Show Us What You're Made Of

*"How many a man has dated a new era
in his life from the reading of a book."*

– HENRY DAVID THOREAU, *WALDEN*

*"Men are anxious to improve their circumstances, but are
unwilling to improve themselves; they therefore remain bound."*

– JAMES ALLEN, AUTHOR

AS A SCHOOLBOY, I remember standing on a freezing, hard pitch in shorts that wouldn't fit for five years, hating the humiliating soccer game I was so inept at that nobody wanted me on their side. I longed for the game to finish so I could thaw out my hands on the white dusty pipes inside. Despite my best efforts to keep out of the action the ball would cruelly roll my way as the teacher shouted, *"Delaney! Show us what you're made of!"*

Men are under pressure, feeling the heat. From the boss, from their family, from impossible stereotypes that the media set up of what a "real" and "successful" man should be or do. We feel compelled to strive toward our own unreachable goals, or the targets others set for us that too often we fail to meet—or the ones that we set ourselves. It's only afterwards we realize they are often Pyrrhic victories, ruinous to our souls, relationships, or character. Instead of being elated, we're deflated again. Wrestling inner doubts and strong temptations, outer struggles and "spare tires," we wonder why we bothered.

It was considered "character building" when as a sixteen-year-old police cadet I was told to go out for a morning run across bitter mountainous areas, before breaking the ice off a stream and submerging myself in subzero waters. No whimpering permitted as your breath was taken away, or push-ups were the punishment. The only character trait this developed in me was a reservoir of latent loathing for sadists with a little power. "*Show us what you're made of!*" rang in my ears again.

Some men climb mountains or base jump to show that they are made of something strong, resilient, and manly. Dissatisfied with life as they know it, others seek sexual conquests, to seek to prove they've "still got it." Trophy wives, company bonuses, or certificates on the wall may paper over the gaps, but not for long. So they keep looking.

Can athletics, acquisitions, or achievements really validate our manhood? Do the 300 workout or "going Paleo" show that we're tough, or sensitive, or whatever we think a "real" man should be like?

The problem is, nothing external shows what we are really made of. If we want to know what we truly are, we need to look inside. To dare to go below the surface. Ask those who live closest to you, who know you best, if you dare. Look in the mirror and ask yourself.

Who is the you that nobody else can see? Who are you when you're under pressure? When you feel the heat?

I believe you also need to ask the God who made you. If you're not there yet, come along for the journey, as I hope to convince you why you will never understand yourself—your limitations and your potential—until you know what He made you of, and for.

Why go to God for answers? For many the thought of religion or church is repulsive. Here in the United Kingdom a recent study suggested 54 percent of men considered themselves atheist or agnostic about the existence of God and nearly 50 percent of men under thirty left church in the last twenty-five years. A survey in the men's magazine *Sorted* found the vast majority of blokes would feel more comfortable visiting the lingerie section of a department store than their local church. What has Christianity got to say to men today?

At least you have a choice. As a little boy I remember being made to go to a church service. As I knelt down at the front, where the sickly smell of incense was strongest, the priest smudged dirt and oil on my head, intoning what I later discovered was a very biblical and also scientifically accurate notion. "Remember you are dust—to dust you shall return." Not a very nice thing to tell a six-year-old. I didn't understand it. Now I do.

In my journey from police officer to church minister I have become very familiar with our mortality. I have stood at thousands of gravesides and realized that the mortality rate is still running at 100 percent. Nobody gets out of here alive! One day the atoms we are made up from—all those protons, neutrons, and croutons—will return to dust. Carbon. All that will remain of you as a carbon-based life form will be some mercury from your fillings and whatever kind of legacy your decisions created, which will really show what you were made of.

COAL MEN

A lump of coal can look quite big and impressive, pretty tough. But, put it under a bit of pressure and it will crumble. Expose it to heat, it will burn. It won't last. I know too often I have been like that. Content with the outward show of looking like I have got it all together. Men are like that. Not some men. Every one.

To protect a vulnerable inner self and project that "I'm doing okay," we put on a show. We don't really know who we are or what it is to be a man and what we want from life. But we know that there must be more than this.

Karl read too many comic books and became convinced he could fly. He was always making some kind of wings or jumping off the prefab buildings at my junior school. When you heard the ambulance siren, it was a safe bet he'd discovered gravity again! From the time we put on a cowboy outfit or climb high to test our super-powers, men become skilled at play-acting. We put on a mask that says everything is happy and okay in my little world, inside of me, with my friends, my family, my work. Occasionally something happens that gives us a buzz or a taste of what we were really made for, that can keep us smiling or distracted for some time. But whether we make the sale, get the girl, or score the goal, eventually men ask, "Now what?" and settle back into the phony role playing.

Do you know why coal is black? Two reasons. First off, it's loaded and mixed up with all kinds of impurities. Second, the structure of the atoms in coal is such that it absorbs light of all wavelengths. It doesn't allow for the transparency that makes a diamond so precious. If we're self-absorbed and we don't let anyone look at what's really going on inside us, we end up in darkness.

Coal men (no offense to anyone in the solid fuel delivery business) have perhaps never known the genuine love of a father in a way that they can understand and relate to. Therefore they are not able to form good relationships with others. They don't understand themselves, so good luck trying to understand others, especially women. Their networks of friendships are often shallow, superficial, and short term. Coal men often end up with their wives divorcing them and their kids not talking to them. They throw themselves into their work to try to show themselves that they are successful somewhere, then die early from stress.

Coal looks impenetrable, but when you examine it up close you can see it's actually full of holes. A coal man has nothing at his center but emptiness. Isolated, lonely, always competing with someone he can never win against (himself). Emotionally stunted, never quite able to make the difference that in his best moments he would like to make in the world—because he would have to deal with his inner world first.

Some coal men are violent, aggressive, patriarchal, resentful, misogynistic, or abusive, embittering those they are supposed to love and protect. Others are New Age luvvies trying to project sensitivity as the appropriate response to fearful feminism's advances, but too weak and afraid of healthy conflict to be respected by women, or to bring the guidance and discipline that are actually required to be a good parent.

Look a little closer. Coal men are male, but not real men. Our society is considerably populated by anxious little boys who never grew up to attain the glorious maturity of maleness that is their true destiny and inheritance. Many men never become who they were truly made to be.

Men commit about 90 percent of all acts of violence.[1] They comprise over 90 percent of the prison population.[2] Tragically, far too many, tired of the outward show and the emptiness of their hearts, decide the best contribution they can make would be to step out of this life sooner rather than later. Males account for three-quarters of suicide deaths, making this a "silent epidemic," the single biggest killer among men under forty-five.[3] From my intake year at high school I can think of five men who never saw their thirties because they topped themselves. They never got to fly.

Coal men, whether of the hard and scary or soft and wimpy variety, have a very hard time getting married (because of fear of commitment) and an even harder time staying married (because of failing to do what they said they were committed to). They are stuck in front of the TV or computer, or stifled in jobs they don't find meaningful. They get into debt for pastimes that don't satisfy or to fill the internal void, buying things to impress friends they are not close to. They make slow progress through the levels of real life they discover no computer game could actually prepare them for.

If you tell me none of this connects with you, you are in denial. Someone may have given you this book for a reason! Years of policing and pastoral experience give me confidence that I am not talking here about extreme cases. Conversations at men's events, at retreats, and in counseling rooms tell me that this is the unspoken truth about the vast majority of men in our society. It's getting worse with every new generation.

Despite outward indications, most men under some kind of pressure will be liable to crumble one way or another. The high cost of low living is that integrity and reputations lie in tatters, with families in ruins.

There but for the grace of God go I—and I really mean that.

ROUGH DIAMONDS

I'm certainly not a perfect man. I'm just an ordinary bloke who discovered the grace of God is more than a saying, it's a reality. I believe there is a better way for us to live passionately, positively—as a perfect man (under construction!).

You may disagree with what I say—but please don't dismiss

anything out of hand, even the stories of Bible characters I'll use throughout. Because the Bible is not just "the good book," it is the most honest book in the world as it tells the stories of its characters' warts and all. If you don't believe in God yet, come along anyway and at least believe that I believe God has a great plan for you. He sees your value and potential. In fact, the heat and the pressure of life are His tools to shape within you something better and brighter.

God didn't make you to be a coal man; they are ten a penny. He sees you as precious and valuable, a rough diamond. Diamonds are not brilliant to look at when first found. The process of diamond recovery sifts out 180 million parts of other material to yield one part of diamond. They differ in color, character, and clarity and can be cut in many ways. The cut greatly impacts how they shine. If a diamond is cut poorly, it will be less luminous and may even be permanently damaged.

We are going to examine six facets of life. If I pushed you on these facets, would you crumble, or shine?

The chapters are about vital issues and will be challenging for every reader. They stand alone as tests of clarity and quality and you might be tempted to skip straight to one that interests you immediately. I know that's what most men do when they read books but I'd be grateful if you didn't. Please check out all sides of the stone in turn.

I'll ask questions now and then. You might want to ponder them or get together with others who are reading the book too. If it helps you engage with it, make notes and use a highlighter. Commit now to finishing the book. Much of what I'm saying only hangs together because of what comes later and I know you're the kind of man who finishes what he starts, right?

Remember, a diamond is still carbon, but deep in the earth's mantle, way below the surface, it has been formed under high-pressure, high-temperature conditions. Rather than crumble or

21

burn up, its very nature is changed. Impurities disappear, and the more that happens the more transparent it becomes. It is reflective rather than self-absorbed. The closer you examine its luster you see that something wonderful and precious shines from within. What matters most is what is at the center.

You can unleash the potential you were created for and intended to live, with nothing to prove, nothing to hide, and everything to live for. Before we continue, I wonder what you would place at the center of your life right now.

Many men would say their family or friends are at the center, which is admirable. Others live lives centered around past failures, or their finances, or their football team. None of those are of course bad in themselves (unless it's Manchester City), but they are not meant to be the center you live from. Try to live with any of those things at the center and you will crumble when the heat is on.

I will tell my own story too and tell you about the best decision I ever made. It affected all the other areas because real change only happens from the inside out. It happened when I decided more than anything else I wanted to become more like the only perfect man. While you might admire a sports or movie star, I say that throughout history the only contender for that title is Jesus Christ.

The following chapters are all to do with your decisions, your actions, and your attitudes. Difficulties with health, parenting, screwing up at work are just symptomatic of the hole we men have in our hearts. We can pretend this doesn't apply to us, put on a happy face or a show of bravado. But when the pressure comes it isn't how much you can bench-press but what is in the center that matters most. That's true core strength.

If I were to sit down one-to-one with you and look you in the eye as I have with many over the years and ask you some questions relating to these areas, you would see how they are linked and intertwined.

For example, what if I were to ask you some deep questions with regard to how you have coped with life's inevitable *failures*?

How you would assess how you really are as a *family* man—as a son, a sibling, a parent, or a husband? How would you rate yourself on that? (Maybe it would be better to get your family in the room and ask them to rate you!)

Men in our society have been radically *under-fathered* for generations, but how you relate to the concept of an earthly father is one of the biggest determinants of your psychological health.

When I joined the police force I worked with men who I knew would die for me if necessary and vice versa. Some of them wrote commendations for this book and I maintain *friendships* with them many years on. True friendship is not a slap on the back or a drink in the pub. Does anybody know your heart, your secret thoughts, what makes you laugh, makes you cry, makes you mad? Would your friendships last over time and under pressure?

Many men are lazy slobs. Others become body-obsessed to the point of idolatry. I maintain a good level of *fitness* for my age by going to the gym regularly and training for the occasional charity challenge. I want to be fit for purpose, to look after my body well, and to be able to give the best that I can give to everything I do.

If I asked you questions in regard to your *finances*, how would you respond? Your bank statement portrays your priorities. What would true financial freedom and balance mean? It will be very interesting to look at that together later. You're in for a few surprises.

SOCKS AND SANDALS AND OTHER SCANDALS

I love being a man, with lots of mates younger and older than me, a wonderful son, and three young grandsons I pray every day will become real men—the way God wants them to be: men who love to laugh, men who love their wives if they marry, men who are strong and yet compassionate, men who pray and act with courage, men who are great in any kind of relationship, men who become great dads, great husbands, great and mighty *men of God.*

Most unchurched men of my acquaintance seem to want to remain that way believing the church is for "women, weirdoes, and wimps."[4] The Christian stereotype turns my stomach as much as yours. That's not what I'm advocating for. God doesn't want you to add a Sunday religious mask to all the others. He wants to give you a cause worth sacrificing for, a battle to win, and brothers to fight alongside you in the war for the world. He wants the very best for you—which is to shape you to be like Jesus Christ.

Somebody asked a sculptor, "How is it that you can take these lumpy pieces of wood full of splinters and knots and can make such beautiful horses from them?"

"Easy," he replied. "I hold them up to the light, I see the stallion inside, and I cut away everything that isn't horse."

In the 1800s, Baptist preacher Charles Spurgeon said, "There has got abroad a notion, somehow, that if you become a Christian you must sink your manliness and turn milksop."[5] No way! God wants to take you on a journey throughout your life where He will use pressures and heat to transform you. Sometimes He may cut away at things you wish He would leave well enough alone. Sometimes He will be very gentle and patient. But the Bible promises that if you put yourself in His hands, if you cooperate with Him, God will shape you in various areas—then one day, when you see the only perfect man, Jesus Christ, you will find that you will recognize Him, you know Him—because you will be like Him.

The word *diamond* comes from a Greek word that means "unbreakable." Inner strength is more important than outer. Are you ready to stop chipping away at life from the outside and learn to live from the inside out? Are you ready to become the man God made you to be?

Eric Delve first explained this great good news in a way that helped me get it and he is fond of reciting the following poem by Henry F. Lyte (who wrote the famous hymn "Abide with Me"). It illustrates very well how God shapes men.

Read it aloud (if you're not on public transport), and if you don't understand it now, one day soon you may.

Whom God Chooses

When God wants to drill a man,
And thrill a man,
And skill a man,
When God wants to mould a man,
To play the noblest part;

When He yearns with all His heart
To create so great and bold a man
That all the world shall be amazed,
Watch His methods, watch His ways!

How He ruthlessly perfects
When He royally elects!
How He hammers him and hurts him,
And with mighty blows converts him

Into trial shapes of clay which
Only God understands;
While his tortured heart is crying
And he lifts beseeching hands!

How He bends but never breaks
When His good He undertakes;
How He uses whom he chooses,
And with every purpose fuses him;
By every act induces him
To try His splendour out—
God knows what He's about.

Go then, earthly fame and treasure!
Come disaster, scorn, and pain!
In Thy service, pain is pleasure;
With Thy favour, loss is gain.

I have called Thee, Abba, Father;
I have stayed my heart on Thee.
Storms may howl, and clouds may gather;
All must work for good to me.

– HENRY F. LYTE

Chapter 2

Fitness

"The first wealth is health."

– RALPH WALDO EMERSON

"We are what we repeatedly do; excellence then is not an act but a habit."

– WILL DURANT, *THE STORY OF PHILOSOPHY*

"Those who go beneath the surface do so at their peril."

– OSCAR WILDE, *THE PICTURE OF DORIAN GRAY*

I'M HIGH WHILE I'm writing this. Don't worry, it's endorphins that do that. I'm feeling good. The sun is shining this morning and I am feeling fresh. My mind is active and full of ideas. I have a positive attitude. I even smell nice. That's what putting yourself through a program of regular exercise can do. An hour ago I really didn't want to do the plyometric circuit (movements combining bodyweight strength movements with dynamic jumps like burpees and squat thrusts) but while it's one of my toughest, sweatiest workout sessions, I know it burns fat, and provides power, balance, stamina, and core stability simultaneously.

The program I followed was designed by a former Royal Marine and tomorrow I'm scheduled for "Hurricanes," which an MMA fighter trainer devised combining sprints and weights. The day after is a rest day, which is just as important.

When it comes to sport I'm a doer rather than a spectator. Living in Manchester makes the odd visit to the "Theatre of Dreams" to watch United something of a must occasionally, but I find I can't switch off and enjoy the match too much, surrounded by men with huge beer guts swearing and yelling at the athletes on the pitch how to play better. Years ago, as a police officer at the height of British football hooliganism, I was put off further when the games became a place to arrest such idiots who wanted to prove their machismo by fighting each other, though the money from the overtime helped.

I have never been keen on watching sports. Some guys can tell you the full lineup of every team, who the manager was in 1971, and what brand of chewing gum he chewed. I have never had the kind of brain that can retain sports trivia. When I was at school the only sporting option was soccer. To meet me now you'd be surprised to learn I was then skinny for my age (I had to run round in the shower to get wet), which contributed to my lack of prowess.

I recently heard *The Tipping Point* author Malcolm Gladwell speculate that the month of the year you are born in makes a big difference as to whether or not you will be successful in such sports. The idiosyncrasies of the selection process used to identify and coach talent matter just as much as the athletes' natural abilities. It is all to do with where you are in the school intake year.

In one study of youth hockey professionals in his book *Outliers*, Gladwell postulates that since youth leagues determine eligibility by calendar year, adolescents born earlier in the year are bigger and more mature than their younger competitors and are often identified as "better athletes," leading to extra coaching and a higher likelihood of being selected for elite leagues. He calls it "accumulative advantage." That's now my excuse for not getting girlfriends at high school, and I am sticking to it.

I count myself fortunate that at the age of sixteen I joined the Police Cadets and was immediately embroiled in all kinds of sports and workouts in the gym, as well as a variety of martial arts. I ate like a horse to fuel the exercise gap and over the next few years I packed on weight and muscle and was soon able to knock people off the ball even though my skills never improved.

Since then I have been fairly disciplined in keeping myself fit. I have run marathons and mountain marathons as well as taken part in a number of short- and middle-distance triathlons. Now in my mid-fifties, I run, swim, and go to the gym every week because I know it's easier to maintain rather than regain good health. I truly believe that looking after your body is not just an optional extra. Taking care of my body, for me, is a major part of what a Christian would call good stewardship. Simply being grateful for and looking after whatever you were given.

The first area we'll examine is **Fitness**. This may come as a surprise to some, especially if you were thinking this is a religious book, but we're invited to remember in the pages of the Bible that everything that we have—the eyes that read this page, your next breath, and the lungs that receive it—is a gift from God. So often it's only when something goes wrong with our health that we become aware of it or grateful for it. What if it matters to God, how we treat everything that we are given: money, family, job, the planet, and of course our bodies? What if everything is spiritual? What if all of our choices matter and are interconnected?

There are two extremes we can fall into with regard to our bodies, fitness levels, and general health. You can become a *worshiper* of your body or swing the other way and be a *waster* of it, neglecting your health. We can deify or destroy ourselves. Either we worship our reflection in the gym mirrors while developing that six-pack, or we wallow in front of the TV drinking one.

The danger with worshiping your body is it leads to pride. You don't have to be kissing your biceps to fall into this camp. Look at your bank statement. How much do you spend on gym membership, suntans, or even plastic surgery to defeat the inevitability of looking older (and the fear of death that is all wrapped up in that)? Weigh that against how much time, energy, and money you put into relationships, and your spiritual well-being. No protein shake feeds your soul.

I'm forced to admit that in the past, when marathon training for example, I have put a big strain on family time and even neglected the people I love most, and for what? A cheap medal or a T-shirt, and the chance to prove something to myself?

Conversely, body wasters don't struggle with pride but sometimes feel guilty instead. Maybe this guilt comes from other people telling them they need to shape up and change something in their lifestyle: stop smoking, drink less, get out more—put the console down and play a real game.

Are you one of those who responds, "Who cares? The guy who invented jogging died young anyway! I'm doing nobody else any harm!" But living on this extreme does affect other people. Those who don't look after themselves end up having to be cared for in hospital or by family instead.

Either extreme of worshiping or wasting will cause tensions in relationships. To be brutally honest, either way the real problem is selfishness.

Bill hasn't seen his wife and kids all week because of the pressures of work. The weekend game is booked. Ignoring the pleas of his family, he throws the golf clubs in the car. "I need to exercise now. You do want me to be healthy, don't you? I'm just looking after myself."

Tom sinks just one more cheeky beer, lights up another ciggy, and turns the volume up to hear and cheer his team. His child wants to kick a ball in the park, but Dad responds, "Later, Son, I'm knackered." He ironically wears a T-shirt bearing the slogan "My Body Is a Temple," not knowing the words come straight from Scripture.

What's God's perspective on how you treat your body? The apostle Paul wrote about this issue to a group of believers in the city of Corinth:

> *Do you not know that your bodies are temples of the Holy Spirit, who is in you, whom you have received from God? You are not your own; you were bought at a price. Therefore honor God with your bodies.*
> 1 Corinthians 6:19–20

When the New Testament was written, Greek philosophy taught that what you did with your body didn't matter. Life here on earth bore little connection to the spiritual. Any relationship to the gods was a purely spiritual thing and had no real bearing on our physical being. In the West today that Greek mindset prevails. We have swallowed the idea that there is a sacred and secular divide.

Imagine how amazed the people in Corinth were then to receive this teaching, that the real God cares very much about all aspects of your life, so what you do with your physical body is a deeply spiritual issue.

The Corinthians knew all about temples. The city was full of magnificent and costly holy sites for pagan worship for the pantheon. Now they are told how God views their bodies: as temples, sacred sites, to be well maintained as a place for deity to dwell.

But it's deeper even than that.

In the fourth century a bishop called Athanasius was called in to adjudicate in the matter of ownership of a boat. A man in Alexandria had made the boat by hand, painted it himself, knew every inch of it. One day he went to the port and it was gone—stolen! Now the man loved the boat, and he scoured the harbors around searching for it. Months became years until one day he saw it, near the Nile. It had been painted a different color, had a new name, but the man knew it was his boat! But a long time had passed and it had gone through many owners, and the man who now possessed it had paid a fair price.

Athanasius decreed that the one who had made it would also have to pay the full price for the boat if he wanted it: "Then nobody will ever be able to say that it doesn't belong to you."

What is God's perspective on your body?

It's not yours. It's His.

Because it's not "my body," I can't just do what I like with it, either to worship it (which is idolatry) or to wastefully abuse it (which is sacrilege). God isn't only interested in the spiritual side of me; the whole package belongs to Him.

We belong to God because He created us in the first place, and then He paid the ultimate price to get us back so nobody can ever say you aren't His. God wants a relationship. God doesn't want us to know some things about Him (as you might know some sporting facts—unlike myself). He wants us to really know Him. Not for an hour on a Sunday, either. He is interested in what happens throughout the week—of which looking after your body is a huge part. How you look after the body you have been given has a great deal to do with whether in this life you will end up living what Jesus calls life "to the full" (John 10:10), and it may also have a bearing on how soon you'll get to experience the next life!

Take, for example, the resting heart rate of a fit man: fifty-two beats per minute.

Time it takes that fit man to log eight million heartbeats: thirty years.

Compare to the resting heart rate of a man the same age who's out of shape: seventy-two beats per minute.

Time it takes an out-of-shape man to log eight million heartbeats: nineteen years.[1]

The heart is a muscle and like any muscle that is exercised, it responds by getting stronger. As your heart gets stronger, your resting pulse rate will fall. Without exercise it will atrophy. Measures like this are more helpful than whether you feel healthy.

Just because you feel okay doesn't mean you are healthy. In one recent survey, "87 percent of men reported being either very active, active or somewhat active."[2] However, here in the UK, simply by virtue of changes in lifestyle, we are 20 percent less active than our forebears in the 1960s[3] and 67 percent of men are overweight or obese.[4]

Fitness is a relative term. It's not just about lifting heavy weights but comprises flexibility, strength, and endurance. Fitness makes a difference to you emotionally, spiritually, and intellectually. Fitness also means "suitability." For a professional athlete it means being ready and at your peak on race day. Fitness for me means the ability to cope with what life throws at me and still having something in reserve.

Can you work all day then be strong enough to change a wheel to help someone in the car park? Could you jog home if you needed to? Do you get out of breath pulling shopping trolleys apart? What are your energy levels like? A woman was asked, "Do you wake up grumpy in the morning?" She replied, "No, he needs to sleep in."

I appreciate that for some of you a disability or illness means you may not be able to immediately get into some high-level physical program. But speaking to the majority now—isn't it true you could maintain or improve your level of fitness if you were to speak to a medical expert and then start on some form of appropriate, regular exercise pattern? I guarantee the results will be more than physical. You'll discover new levels of self-respect, determination, and well-being. Could you make a change for the better today in one of the three areas most important for fitness: exercise, correct nutrition, and rest?

It's never too late. My grandfather started walking five miles a day when he was sixty. Now he's ninety-eight years old and we have no idea where he is.

I used to live near an armed forces rehabilitation center and they shared the local pool I went to. To see some of these men—double amputees and so on—not giving up but pushing themselves to make the best of a terrible situation was so inspiring to me. They refuse to just lie there. Many got involved in running marathons, or Paralympic events, doing what others would view as impossible. They believed, "It ain't over until it's over" and epitomized "Who dares wins." So if you're a couch potato, what's your excuse? There may be a few things you can't do, but there are hundreds of things you can do.

> "If you always put limits on everything you do, physically or anything else, it will spread into your work and into your life. There are no limits—there are only plateaus—and you must not stay there, you must go beyond them."
>
> **BRUCE LEE**

WHAT FITNESS MEANS FOR YOU

I'm not saying you should let any kind of fitness program monopolize your life. But any of us can set a goal and then push ourselves—where? Beyond the limits of our expectations!

You must decide what fitness means for you, what you want to be fit for, and then how much time you can afford to spend on it. You don't need a crash diet or an impossible dream, you just need a purpose, a plan, and program to follow for life. A plan to keep fit anywhere at any age with minimal time and equipment is achievable. Right now thirty to forty minutes of challenging exercise five days a week keeps me smiling, slim(ish), and sexy for my wife.

Your fitness aims are probably different than mine but the most important parts about any program are:

- to be honest with yourself—decide what's achievable
- to enjoy yourself—you are more likely to stick with it
- to challenge yourself—stretching yourself will keep you from boredom, set a goal
- to rest yourself—recovery is as important as training.

BE SAFE

Of course, the first and most important thing to do before embarking on any kind of fitness program is to see your doctor for a checkup, especially if you are overweight, have high blood pressure (hypertension), any kind of irregular heartbeat, or a history of any kind of medical condition that may affect your mobility. Go to a running shop to get correctly fitting shoes for your biomechanics so you don't get injured walking out the door! Wearing proper sports clothing will get you in the right state of mind from the start.

You have to start from where you are. Assess your level of

fitness right now, then track your changes and you will stay motivated. Body fat scales are more helpful than normal scales. They calculate your body mass index (BMI) and muscle weighs heavier than fat (that's what I keep telling myself), so while you get fitter and leaner you may not necessarily weigh less by following a fitness plan. Do you have any addictions? Fitness can help replace them—it's a positive addiction. Be sensible about your diet but don't obsess about calories—eat whole foods and stop when you're full. The best exercise many of us could do is push-ups—push up from the table before dessert arrives.

There are various websites where you can predict your life expectancy based on your lifestyle now. Some of you need to do this quickly—it may mean you have to make dramatic changes or read a lot faster to finish the book!

Many people I talk to seem to be under the impression that getting fit takes a long time. I don't think it does. You can see dramatic improvements from a regular and consistent workout pattern that only lasts half an hour, a few days a week—as long as you are working efficiently. I know that because I have seen it in my own life, though it does get harder to see results as we get older.

What's your next step? Following a program with a mixture of resistance, exercises, stamina building, and aerobic fitness will give you that great feeling that you only get as your body releases endorphins from exercise. Work to fatigue, not all-out failure, which elevates levels of the stress hormone cortisol, reducing the body's ability to repair itself.

You don't have to spend hours a day in a gym trying to get fit. Despite what a whole industry will say to the contrary, you don't even need to join a gym! Whatever your age, whether you are fit or unfit right now, it's time to go to another level, and to do that you just need to learn the skills necessary to get and maintain fitness then get on with it.

BE PREPARED

Baden-Powell's, "be prepared," motto was right. It is important that we schedule regular workouts and rest days too. A familiar routine will increase your chances to stick with it. Ninety percent of success is just showing up—with your trainers on!

Some say that it is good to train in the morning because testosterone levels are higher. None of that really matters. What counts is that you pick a time that works for you. Put your training gear together so you're ready to go. Don't put it off till tomorrow. You may feel like you can't be bothered, but if you have planned in your schedule time to train then it is good to make a pact with yourself and say, "Whether or not I feel like doing it I am going to start, and keep on starting."

I find it useful to give myself occasional treats if I have not slipped away from my program, but have carried on with it, because what defeats a lot of us is that you won't see a difference overnight. It takes time to reach your goals, but consistency yields surprising results.

BE REALISTIC

You may not run the Marathon des Sables next year. You may not even want to carry on tomorrow. Remember, some days are harder than others. That's life. As a runner I know that one day you will feel like you can run forever (believe me, it will come) and other days you will feel like you are dragging the carcass of a dead moose up a hill. Don't give up.

Make sure you drink a lot of water, have a good low-fat diet, and get proper nourishment. Every health gain is worth the discipline it takes to achieve it. I used to smoke and though I know it's stupid and disgusting, I have to admit there are times I still crave a cigar, but do you know what? I crave a healthy life more. Say yes to the right things and no to the wrong things, one day at a time. Stick with it and you will see the results, and so will others.

One of the spin-off benefits from exercise is that you will get happy. You will not look like a zombie movie extra. So often, like today, I've finished my exercise feeling energized and motivated to get on with all the other things I have to do in life. I find innovative thoughts for my work, and creative ideas for my talks click into place almost out of nowhere. Science has proven that exercise reduces tension, depression, and anger. Even twenty minutes can boost your mood for hours. If you become fitter your body will in essence detox itself. You will cut down on your bad habits. Not because you have to, but because you want to. The temple starts to clean itself.

The Bible says you are "fearfully and wonderfully made" (Ps. 139:14). The human body was designed as the pinnacle of God's artistry. He created you a rough diamond, to showcase His glory, then paid the highest price imaginable to buy you back—so nobody can deny you belong to Him. Therefore, honor God with your body.

Would you say you err toward being a body worshiper or a body waster?

Exercise deficiency threatens your overall health and mental well-being, and shortens your life span. By meeting recommended levels of physical activity, your risk of heart disease, stroke, and type 2 diabetes is reduced.

Doctors recommend that adults should do 150 minutes (at least) of physical activity a week.[5]

Those aged eighteen and under should be doing an hour each day.

Are you doing enough to be fit for life?

What's your next move?

Chapter 3

Finances

*"All I ask is the chance to prove
that money can't make me happy."*
– ATTRIBUTED TO SPIKE MILLIGAN

*"Money is not the most important thing in the world.
Love is. Fortunately, I love money."*
– ATTRIBUTED TO JACKIE MASON

"Our yearnings will always exceed our earnings."
– J. JOHN

I WAS NINETEEN, and it was a hot day at the training school. I'd been doing hard exercise all morning and had a big lunch. Then we had a boring talk lined up, someone from the police's pensions and finance department with a degree in total monotony, coming to tell us about money. A practical session about avoiding debt . . . living within your means . . . spending and investing wisely . . . blah, blah, blah. I lasted about ten minutes.

I thought I'd close my eyes, just for a few moments.

I got away with it. I just looked like I was thinking, hard. Wow, it's stuffy in this room. Drone . . . drone . . . pensions . . . savings . . . taxes. Just a few more seconds with my eyes closed, then I'll nod and look like I'm thinking, really pondering deeply.

What seemed like two seconds later, I was prodded by John, the copper next to me. He was smiling widely. I smiled back. Until I saw the glaring face of the boss who was giving the talk. Not impressed.

Why? Surely it was only a matter of moments? Then I felt the large damp patch on the front of my shirt. It turns out I'd been gone about twenty minutes. Fully gone. Loudly snoring, sniffing, and (yes) slobbering, my head rolling back and forward and from side to side like Homer Simpson in church. It's safe to say looking back, the subject of money and finances didn't interest me much.

This was the eighties, the decade of decadence. It cost good money to really dress like a fool back then. Around the same time I began to earn good money. I went into a cool men's clothes shop where I ogled the baggy shirts and Bowie trousers I craved. I was greeted by a mullet-wearing bloke with the sleeves of his jacket rolled up, who looked like an extra from *Miami Vice*. I recognized him—a few years above me at school, this guy now worked here and really looked the part (as I reflect on it now I won't tell you which part).

At school he had never even spoken to me. Now he took a very keen interest in showing me the latest styles, many of which really suited me (he said). I had only gone in for a leather tie, but he showed me a nice two-tone suit with the smallest lapels imaginable and some great shoes to go with it. I was worried about not being able to afford it until he kindly offered me a store card so I could take it away, get a discount on what I'd bought, and then make "easy payments" on it. Bargain! I rolled the sleeves up and wore it all weekend in the nightclubs. But I paid for it for years.

It wasn't until I got married that someone far more sensible than me said she was going to do some plastic surgery, cut up that card, and pay it all off—ouch!—not just make minimum payments on the interest. I slowly realized that the shopkeepers and salespeople were not really my friends at all. They were not in business to help me except to relieve me of my hard-earned cash to give themselves a nice fat bonus. It's all too easy these days to become unbalanced in the area of your finances, and I have to watch myself very closely even now, to stop that from happening.

BALANCING ACT

Some of you know you really need to read this chapter on finances, but you don't want to. You're tempted to not read this chapter, for one of two reasons.

The first is that you feel trapped and uncomfortable talking about how you relate to money, because you and your money have a relationship. Some of you are thinking, "Yeah, divorce!" Actually it's not meant to be just a two-way relationship because the Bible talks about a three-way relationship between you, your money, and God. As with any relationship, if you get it wrong there's frustration, fear, and pain. Get it right, and there's joy.

"We needed something to worship and something to believe in and have long since swapped God with Gucci. We have been living beyond our means, in debt beyond our ability to pay, in the naive but hopeful belief that this would be the bubble that would never burst."
NEIL LAWSON, *All Consuming*

Right now you know exactly what J. John means when he says, "Just when you started to make ends meet, somebody moved the ends!" You're not balancing the books. You think saving money means you got it in a sale. Read on, my friend—been there, bought the T-shirt, even though I already have lots of T-shirts.

The second reason you might be tempted to skim this section is because you're doing okay, relatively speaking. Of course a little extra income wouldn't hurt—even J. D. Rockefeller, when he was asked how much money would it take to make him happy, said, "Just a little bit more." Please bear with me, because even though you've got money in the bank—you may yet have to learn the most important thing about money.

I remember from physics that when there is balance, there's less friction. I was also taught that being out of balance results in acceleration, until something happens to reestablish equilibrium. The laws of balance apply not just for the tightrope walker, ballet dancer, or gymnast—they also apply in the area of our finances. You go to the ATM and you want to check your what? Your balance.

Certain principles will help us to balance anything, resulting in less friction. Break the laws of financial balance and you'll end up broke. When things get out of balance they can accelerate out of control very quickly and affect an individual, a business, a bank, or a nation. As I write, my own nation's debt is 94.90 percent of its GDP.[1]

Perhaps you have major personal debt issues. If so, you need support. Ever tried to balance on one leg? Harder than it looks. Now get someone to just put one finger on your elbow to support you a little and it's far easier. If you're seriously out of balance then you need support. Just having someone come to stand alongside you really makes a difference psychologically. You're not alone.

The last thing you want is one of these loan shark companies on the TV that masquerade as quick fix solutions but just land you in yet more debt at extortionate interest. I highly recommend that you contact a charitable organization like CAP (Christians Against Poverty) for genuinely free support that can get you headed toward a debt-free future as it has for thousands of others. My church partners with CAP and has also established a job club and various other initiatives to help people who would otherwise struggle alone, and we regularly hear that someone locally has become debt-free through their help, at which point I do a cartwheel!

WHAT'S YOUR AIM?

If a gymnast sets out to balance across a beam, they won't look down at their feet. They focus on a fixed point in the distance. Someone stretching in the gym in a Pilates class gets told when balancing to "Aim at a spot on the wall." If not, you fall over. You have to have an aim to be in balance. A good financial advisor's first question would ask you what your aim for your money is.

Some people aim to **make as much as they can**. You can quickly end up way off-balance like that. Some of us guys use net worth as a measure of self-worth. A philosopher called Epicurus once said, "To whom little is not enough, nothing is enough." You can always think of more things to do with more money, and if that's where you look for contentment it will be a carrot on a stick, always just out of reach. If continued accumulation drives your life, you will never be satisfied and you will inevitably have relational issues.

The Bible never says money is evil; it's just a commodity of exchange that can be used for good or ill. What it does say is, "The *love* of money is the root of all kinds of evil" (1 Tim. 6:10 NLT, emphasis mine). You may have the Midas touch, but you know how his story ended! It's madness to think that more money equates to more happiness. Who's more happy, the man with ten million or the man with ten kids? The man with ten kids, because he has more than enough!

Some men will answer that their financial aim is **to provide for their loved ones**. Noble words. But often misguided. Savoo.co.uk recently commissioned a survey of two thousand five hundred British working dads, to study their attitudes toward family life. When asked to identify the roles they perceived as their key responsibilities within their own family unit, three-quarters of those questioned identified themselves more as a breadwinner than as a father. In the same survey, three-quarters said they wished they spent less time working and more time with their kids.[2] They need to have a word with themselves!

Providing for your loved ones is a great thing to do—in fact the Bible commands it. In The Message version, 1 Timothy 5:8 puts it very strongly: "Anyone who neglects to care for family members in need repudiates the faith." But that goes way beyond money. We all know someone who was good at looking after their family financially but not relationally. Kids want our presence more than our presents!

Your aim may be **to save a lot of money.** In Luke 12:13–21 Jesus told a parable about a character we call the rich fool as a sobering reminder that one day you will be pushing up the daisies instead of piling up the interest, and who'll get it all then? Rainy days happen, so saving is wise. But it's not going to bring real security or joy in your life or your finances. Riches can be gone quicker than you can say "Ebenezer Scrooge" regardless of where you invest in this life, and you won't be much fun to live with if all you want to do with your money is save it! True financial wisdom doesn't just extend ten or twenty years into the future—it takes account of eternal realities.

Your aim could be simply, **"Spend, spend, spend!"** It's how most people live these days, as we've moved on from keeping up with the Joneses to trying to keep up with the Kardashians, as the advertisers promised we could. Living on 110 percent of your income or more is a recipe for misery and disaster, but even with a global recession in the not-so-distant past, we let ourselves off the hook by pointing the finger at greedy bankers and bent politicians. But we spend the money. We bought the stuff, defined ourselves by it. We shop and shop, as the economy drops.

FINANCIAL FREEDOM

Can I suggest a great aim for your finances? To be financially free. The picture most would have of being financially free is to do whatever they want. That sounds like a good aim, but it's only halfway to heaven.

We all know stories of people who have multiple millions and yet their lives end up a train wreck. You probably think if you had that kind of money you'd be clever enough not to waste it like that. Yet households here in Britain spend, on average, £1.9million in a lifetime.[3] You can make all you can, splurge all you can, save all you can, look after your family—all well and good. But good enough?

How about this as an aim? To not have to worry about money, because you simply have enough to do whatever God wants. Impossible? That was the way Jesus Christ lived during His time on the earth and He said we can live like that too. He made this the centerpiece of his financial advice: "Your heavenly Father knows that you need them. But seek first his kingdom and his righteousness, and all these things will be given to you as well. Therefore do not worry about tomorrow, for tomorrow will worry about itself" (Matt. 6:32–34).

Whether thinking about saving, spending, investing, or giving, the Bible says consistently: if you want true financial balance, your aim should be to put God first in that three-way relationship with money. We looked in the last chapter at how an important facet of your life is to look after the body God gave you well, which will reap all kinds of benefits. The same principle that governs your health applies to your wealth. God gives you 100 percent of everything, and expects you to look after it all well, and give some of it back.

A phrase in one of the Church of England prayer books reminds regular worshipers of this aim every Sunday. It comes right out of words in the Old Testament, spoken by one of the richest and wisest men who ever lived, King David, on the day he gave away literally tons of his own gold to fund building work on the temple in Jerusalem. He beautifully summed up his attitude with regard to wealth and how he aimed to use it:

> Yours, Lord, is the greatness, the power, the glory, the splendour, and the majesty; for everything in heaven and on earth is yours. All things come from you, and of your own do we give you.
> **Church of England, *New Patterns for Worship***

God gave everything to you in the first place. You only ever give back. As these words say, ALL things come from Him. So anything we give back to Him or to help others is a natural and grateful response to His generosity and love.

Great nineteenth-century British statesman John Bright is attributed with this acerbic assessment of then prime minister Benjamin Disraeli: "He is a self-made man, and worships his creator."[4] However much we make, we are not self-made at all. Anything you ever had, anyone who has ever been able to do anything, whatever the achievement, owes that accomplishment to the God who enabled it. That's what David realized as he looked at all his "stuff."

Even though from a human perspective, David had led well, fought hard, and made some courageous decisions and sacrifices to amass the possessions, position, and prestige he enjoyed, he was humble enough not to take the credit. He knew God was at work—in an up-front way or behind the scenes—to give him "all things." So, this earthly king sought God's kingdom first. He aimed at being generous, grateful, and faithful with what he was entrusted.

Everything changes in our relationship to money when we get that same perspective. Do you want to get out from under the burden, fear, and worry of having to be in charge of your financial future, so you can have joy? How do you get that? Transfer the ownership. Put God in charge. Do it today. Put God back in charge of it all. Even if I'm great with money, I don't know what tomorrow brings. It can all go quicker than you can say "Chinese stock market crash." Transfer ownership: put back in first place the God who supplies it in the first place.

I know that I have been given a lot to look after but whether I have more or less I have a lot less to worry about when I remind myself that I'm not really the owner of it. Everything I have is on loan to me, for the short amount of time I am on earth. People who have this perspective have a different aim for their treasure, time, and talents. They say to God, "All things come from You." Their aim is to please Him with all of it. That's where I believe true financial freedom starts, as we don't worry but do what God says, with all He gives us.

God doesn't need your money. A preacher named Andy Stanley says, "God doesn't want anything from you—he wants something for you!" If God rules your life, not greed, need, or want, you start living as a financially free person, free to be generous.

God's aim is for us to honor Him with His money, to manage all of it in a way that honors Him. This is what it means to be a steward, to look after what belongs to another, the way He would want me to. As I do that, I have found He meets all my needs. I make decisions in regard to my income, expenditure, saving, giving, pensions, the same as you do—but the filter question now is not "What do I want?" Rather it's, "God, how do I honor You?"

ACT YOUR WAGE

Ignorance is not bliss! So often over the years I've met with people who don't want to open their bank statements or credit card bills—dreading another phone call, they bury their head in the sand. Burying doesn't work, budgeting does. You have to know where your money is going so you can decide where you want it to go in the future.

It may help you to then get out the cash you think you will need and use that instead of cards. I know that's countercultural these days. Banks and retailers have combined to try to make us feel that cash is somehow old hat. Why? Well, I've noticed something about spending: cash hurts, plastic doesn't. If I go into a shop and have to pay cash, I don't get that money back, or I walk out with less of it. But if I pay by card, it comes back looking just the same—it doesn't even shrink! The lie is that it's not costing you anything, yet.

What is your money going toward month by month? If you make decisions that commit all your income to servicing debts or a lifestyle you can't afford, you'll never know the thrill of proving that what Jesus said is true, that it's better to be a giver than a taker. You will find it impossible to be generous when others have a need or you feel you have an opportunity to help someone with a God-honoring vision. Even if your heart is moved, your purse can't stretch. It's already gone, or going. It's now a sofa, a new phone, a TV. If you've spent it, you can't choose to give it or save it now, because a previous choice prevents it. I know it's obvious but we act like it's not. You may have the best of intentions but decisions trump intentions every time. Your decisions will tie you up, or set you free.

Two thousand years ago, Jesus Christ said something incredibly insightful about money, still every bit as appropriate to people in our day:

> *For where your treasure is, there your heart will be also.*
> Matthew 6:21

What is your treasure? Where is it? There's a treasure map that's easy to follow and it's called your bank statement. Whatever one might say, it points straight to wherever your true treasure is. Your money shows where your heart goes. If our heart is in a particular company, we'll buy shares. If our heart is in a particular team, we'll buy a season ticket. So once again we find this is a deeply spiritual issue.

Jesus talked about money like it was a spiritual entity that could act as an opposing force. He used an Aramaic word to describe it, *mammon*, a false god that imprisons those who serve it. It can control every part of your life. Every decision. Mammon can become another master and Jesus went on to say, "No one can serve two masters. Either you will hate the one and love the other, or you will be devoted to the one and despise the other. You cannot serve both God and money" (Matt. 6:24).

Do you only want God in charge and master of your money when it all goes wrong? A lot of people have that reaction when they have money problems—they really want God to be in charge then, but they were happy to try to be in charge up to that point. There is a battle for your heart being waged every day and it's all to do with your treasure. This is a tension that will never go away while we're here on this earth. Who are you serving now? Are you going to be possessed by your possessions? Is money the deity that decides your destiny? Will your future security and hope lie in ambition, accumulation, and acquisition? Do you want God to serve you by helping you in that pursuit, or will you serve God and surrender ownership of everything back to Him? You can't have it both ways.

THE SECRET OF FINANCIAL HAPPINESS

Our culture makes us feel like we never have enough. Edmund Burke wrote in 1756, "The great error of our nature is, not to know where to stop, not to be satisfied with any reasonable acquirement . . . but to lose all we have gained by an insatiable pursuit after more."[5] We forget how fortunate we are. We have enough, and enough to spare, and yet still we hanker for more.

The greatest financial lesson we can ever learn is to be content. The apostle Paul wrote from prison to some friends and said:

> *I have learned to be content whatever the circumstances. I know what it is to be in need, and I know what it is to have plenty. I have learned the secret of being content."*
> Philippians 4:11–12

What's the secret? How did he learn it? The hard way! Contentment's never found by consuming more. You never get more content by having more. I want more: bigger, newer, better, best—always comparing, rarely content, but God wants to teach me contentment. How? By giving me everything I want, when I want it? Is that going to teach me contentment?

Some parents do that with their kids. We have a word for such children: spoiled.

Paul says he learned contentment. He learned it, because it's not natural. We don't learn to be content with what we have, until we learn to be content with what we don't have. That's how God teaches contentment. I never really had to think about money all those years I was in the police, then for three years at seminary we learned about contentment by doing without. And our family also learned all about God's sufficiency and miraculous provision too!

Do you know what's the number one enemy of contentment? Comparison. Comparing to others takes all my contentment away. Jesus said it's like the birds and flowers. Are they worrying? No. Why? They're not comparing.

Birds don't say, "You got more worms than me!"

Daisies don't say, "I wish I was a rose! Then I could be happy."

Why?

Because they can't talk.

But if they could, they'd be happy to be what God made them

to be! Comparison robs your contentment. You know this! You get a new job, you're chuffed—until you find out somebody else got better perks, the bigger office.

You're thinking, "What a great home God's given us!" Then you visit your friends and their house is twice the size, and now your house stinks.

I'm making travel arrangements to go to Haiti again soon with my wife, Zoe, with a great charity called Compassion UK. We'll visit the projects we've helped and two of the kids we sponsor out there.

What if you compared your home to theirs in Haiti? A one-room tin shack shared by the whole family that you just moved into after years in a leaky plastic-sheet tent provided after the earthquake in 2010. We compare instead with somebody who has more, and it takes your joy away. We are not just to feel bad about that, but to act in revolutionary fashion for the sake of justice and equality. As Mohandas Gandhi, who admired Jesus and was inspired by Him, said, "If we could change ourselves, the tendencies in the world would also change."[6]

Do you want to see the world change? Start by going to howrichami.givingwhatwecan.org/how-rich-am-i and put in how much income you have been given. As I write, the average UK worker earns £25,971 per annum.[7] You may earn substantially more or less, but about 9.2 percent of the world population is living on less than $1.90 per day.[8]

Think back over the last year, and add up the total amount of money that you've given away to charity (the church, the poor, or whatever causes get dear enough to your heart to be near enough to your wallet). Now work out what percentage of your income—all that God entrusted to you—that equates to. Most of us think we are a lot more generous than we actually are. Buying your round does not really count here. The average American gives "2.1% of their disposable income to charity."[9] How could Paul, while awaiting being put on trial for his life, write in the same letter both "I have lost all things" and "Do not be anxious about anything" (Phil. 3:8, 4:6)? Paul was from a wealthy family; he had his own business—on occasion some people kept him in jail just hoping he'd give them a lot of money to get out (see Acts 24:26). He says, "I've been rich. I've been poor. Now I'm content either way" (see Phil. 4:12). How? He set his contentment bar much lower than ours.

In another letter he encouraged a young man he mentored: "If we have food and clothing, we will be content with that" (1 Tim. 6:8). That's the bar for his contentment; he decided that's enough. What is enough for you and me? Paul says it is if you've got enough to eat today and something on your back. It doesn't even talk about houses. I watch the news and see refugees heading toward my country, leaving war-torn places in inflatable dinghies or dying crammed in trucks—with nothing. They don't have enough. But I have more than enough. If I get my comparisons right.

If you've ever traveled around the world to anywhere approaching the poverty line, not just on a package holiday where they shield you from it but up close with the reality—then surely you are aware of how fortunate you are. If you're living indoors, have food on the table, and a change of clothes to wear then actually you're in a massively privileged minority in global terms. *Daily Mail* reports that we throw away 42 percent of purchased food a day in my nation.[10] According to worldhunger.org, about 3.1 million children die every year from malnutrition,[11] while we have to carry fat dogs to the vet. And UNICEF claims that one in three children in the world are stunted because they haven't got enough. I have more than enough!

CONSUMPTION OR CONTRIBUTION?

I visited a recently widowed lady to discuss details for the funeral of her husband. This man was probably Ivy's oldest member. We are a young church but for forty years Doug loved Ivy and served here and in the city, and since his teens when he gave his life to following Jesus he had tirelessly worked and prayed for the people of China. Finally, peacefully at home, at the age of eighty-five, he went to be with the Lord. The Salvation Army calls it being "promoted to glory"—he went to where his treasure is.

Now our biggest concern is where will we find somewhere big enough to hold all the people who love him and are grateful for him. What a legacy! People from all over the world, especially the Chinese people he loved so much and served so faithfully all his life, want to gather now to thank God for Doug's contribution.

Will you measure your life by its duration or donation, by its consumption or its contribution, by the loot—or the legacy?

There would be more than enough if we did what Jesus said and became like little children and then learned to share. If God blessed us with more than enough, let's aim to be content, and make a bigger contribution.

RATE YOURSELF

In a consumer society most people are mostly concerned with consumption. Rate yourself 1 to 100 instead according to these three Cs.

CONCERN

What injustices in the world do you care enough about to give time or money toward changing? Zero would be "nothing much if anything"; 100 would be shedding blood, laying down your life for it, the kind of concern most graphically shown for us at the cross.

CONTENTMENT

Some of you wish there was more than 100 on the scale, in which case you're not really getting this. Give yourself a mark on how content you are with what you have, right now. How much do you agree with the statement "I have learned that I have more than enough"?

CONTRIBUTION

If the first two were kind of hard for you to quantify, I understand that. It's hard to accurately gauge them, but for this last one, in financial terms anyway, you should know. God knows. He knows your contribution. Nobody else needs to, but you should know. However much or little you give back or give away, God keeps giving you 100 percent. Some people consume 110 percent of it or more for themselves and their needs—a recipe for financial misery. Some of you take a percentage and save it. The Bible commends that as wisdom. Not hoarding, but saving.

But roughly how much out of all that 100 percent God gives you do you give back to Him? How can you live so you leave a greater legacy?

PRACTICAL EXERCISE

For the next few weeks, before trying to do anything differently with your money, as you think about different financial aims, being content to make a contribution, being financially free because you transferred the ownership of everything back to God, notice what you spend money on this week. Even the little things.

Write down everything you spend for a week or two. Many people have found it helpful to try to live with just cash to do this and realized how much easier that makes it to stay balanced, though the world around us seems to conspire against that! Review it at the end of each week. If you don't know where it's coming from, you'll wonder where it went.

Chapter 4

Family

"A man should never neglect his family for business."
– ATTRIBUTED TO WALT DISNEY

HOW MANY of the following are real titles of country and western songs?

"Mama Get the Hammer (There's a Fly on Papa's Head)"
"Her Teeth Was Stained, but Her Heart Was Pure"
"How Can I Miss You—if You Won't Go Away?"
"I Changed Her Oil, She Changed My Life"
"I Don't Know Whether to Kill Myself or Go Bowling"
"I Don't Want Your Body if Your Heart's Not in it"
"I've Got Tears in My Ears from Lying on My Back in My Bed
    While I Cry Over You"

I'll give the answer, and the tenuous reason for the quiz, later.

THE MOST IMPORTANT THING ABOUT FAMILY

I was asked at short notice to write an article for a men's magazine on the subject of family. The deadline was just days away and we were getting ready to go away on a short family holiday.

I wanted to say yes. I love writing. Churchill said the secret to being a writer is to apply glue to your backside and get in the chair. I decided I could squeeze the time in to write the article, along with all the other things I had to do for work, before the holiday.

All it would take was less helping at home, less time with Zoe and the kids, more stress for myself and everyone else, offloading more pressure onto my team, and locking myself away in the study. I could put a "do not disturb" notice up to tell them and myself that I was doing "the work of the Lord." I could probably even make it so they'd all feel guilty if they tried interrupting such important work. I'm a past master at that.

But I was defeated by the subject: family.

As I started to write I remembered how I came close to losing my family by such shenanigans years ago. I nearly train-wrecked my life to chase the top grade in a qualification I later discovered nobody really cares about. Not wanting to repeat the mistake, I emailed the editor with a great phrase I once read Paul Newman said he used to use when he wanted to turn something down politely but firmly: "Sorry, but it's impossible for me right now."

It was very hard for me as a man who, like you, wants to feel needed, important, and significant. To press "send" on an email admitting to not actually being omnipotent. It was tough to say no, especially to a friend. It was hard to say no to more of "God's work" in order to say "yes" to family time. Family means different things to different people—for me now it's mainly my wife, three kids, and three grandsons. When this happened the kids were younger and the idea I would be sleeping with a granny seemed preposterous. How time flies!

And what if my family is my first and most important work and ministry? In the end it would not matter too much if my kids never read another article I wrote, or listened to another of my sermons. They read and listen to my life.

The problem is, I can quantify how many hours I put into my job, but I can never quantify how well I'm doing as a dad, or as a husband. Perhaps that's why many guys end up putting their all into their work, laying everything on that altar, because it all counts tangibly. In contrast, we never really know how well we're doing in the area of family. There's no tick sheet.

I sent the email, but the subject of family still ticked away in the back of my mind. Because I wasn't writing an article about family I could actually sit down with mine for our evening meal, and I asked, "What do you think the most important thing about family is?"

After a few moments' thought, my daughter Hannah volunteered, "We need to remember that the other people in the family are actually people themselves—not just roles in relation to me."

I asked her to explain that a little. "Well," she said, "it's only been in the last couple of years that I've come to realize—you're not just 'my dad' and Mum's not just 'my mum,' but you are separate people—with your own ideas, and lives, and everything."

Wow. How often have I thought of her as "my daughter" rather than "Hannah"? Too often.

TREE PEOPLE

One day Jesus miraculously healed a blind man. How He did it is fascinating. He took him away from the crowd so He could give him undivided individual attention, and prayed for him. Then He asked the man what he could see.

"I see people; they look like trees walking around" (Mark 8:24).

Now I have to admit, if that were the Anthony Delaney Traveling Ministry Healing Crusade, I would have called that a result! For less than that a lot of people have got their own channel on Christian TV, put a white suit on, and charged big money for a miracle handkerchief.

Jesus wasn't satisfied.

My wife calls me "Half-a-job Joe." I kid myself if I think it's affectionate. She says it because of all the partly completed projects I am surrounded by, especially DIY—which when I make things, stands for "Drat!", "Idiot!", and "Yelling!" (that's the non-swearing version).

Jesus, the master carpenter of Nazareth, is not happy to do half a job. He would not want a man to only be able to see other people looking like trees. Jesus wanted him to see other people as people. Just as Hannah does. So, in no rush, He prayed for him a second time.

We all need to slow down if we are going to make that unhurried second touch, second word, and second prayer, so we can see people as people, especially in our family—however your family is constituted.

Too often I'm chasing my to-do list, checking my phone, or changing my status. I'm rushing around and juggling so many projects that the people closest to me, who I say I love the most, get blurred by my myopia because I'm too easily distracted by what became more important in the moment. This incorrect focus is perilous to me and ruinous to my family.

DEAL OR NO DEAL?

James (not his real name) used to be in marketing until he got into gambling. Highly intelligent and creative, he was earning more money than any of his peers. One night after a brainstorming session for another great new product they would get us to buy, his brain stormed out. A few of the blokes were going to a casino. He won big that night, and the dopamine rush to his brain was all it took. He was hooked. He didn't even want to fight it. The buzz was too strong. But it didn't last. What else could give him such pleasure? He went looking.

He didn't literally put his kids on the roulette table and see them spin off, but he might as well have done. Nobody who shares his name will now share the time of day with him. He lost his wife, because of too many one-night stands. After a while he cut out buying drinks and thinking up the chat-up lines and just paid for sex.

When I first came to lead Ivy Church he used to come along occasionally; he told me he liked the music and liked the people because they liked him. But he liked crack cocaine best. I talked with him a few times about what he thought about God and he said, "God loves me anyway." He told me drugs aren't bad, they are "nice." They were what mattered most to him.

I hadn't seen him for a long time, then one day I sat with him while he waited for a bus. He had just missed one because he couldn't even start to run for it. I wouldn't have let him on my bus if I'd been the driver. He's about my age but looked twenty years older, and I'm looking rough this morning.

He told me where he'd been. On what he called a "super binge."

The last item of value from his former life as a family man was a little apartment. He sold it just after Christmas and spent the tens of thousands it released on an epic bender of hard drugs and warm women. A month of living like hell—no wonder he looked like it. The bus would take him to a squat where someone was letting him sofa surf for a few days.

"So now you have got nothing?!"

His few remaining black teeth showed widely. "Well, I've always got God, haven't I?"

At that point he only ever got the grace part of the Christian message. But not amazing grace. Amazing grace *saves* a wretch like me. He wanted enough to be saved for the next life but not enough to make any difference in this one. He wanted enough to know he's unconditionally loved but not enough love to give away to anyone else.

I've prayed with a number of people at their deathbed conversions. Maybe that's your plan too. Live like hell then ask for heaven with your last breath. If God is real He has to forgive you—that's His job. I have some shocking news for you about that in the final chapter.

"God loves me anyway, Anthony," James said, and I had to go some way toward agreeing with him theologically, but I also wanted to smack him one. I know that's not a pastorally sensitive response. How did I slip through the net for vicar training?

I didn't wait for the next bus with him. I was too annoyed. Later I couldn't get him out of my mind—the waster! The waste of money in a world of need. The waste of potential. The waste of a life. The waste of his family.

It was still burning inside me the next day, but when I read my Bible that morning, I found God challenged my thinking. Reading the Bible regularly will regularly do that.

SMOKE AND MIRRORS

I read the memoirs of a king—Solomon. Scripture says he was the wisest and richest man who had ever lived to that point; the man who had everything. In the end he came up empty. He started on a quest to try to find fulfillment by self-gratification; he had the means at his disposal for a grand experiment like that. I'm glad he wrote up the results so we could learn the lesson from him, rather than the hard way:

I said to myself, "Let's go for it—experiment with pleasure, have a good time!" But there was nothing to it, nothing but smoke. What do I think of the fun-filled life? Insane! Inane! My verdict on the pursuit of happiness? Who needs it? . . . Everything I wanted I took—I never said no to myself. I gave in to every impulse, held back nothing. I sucked the marrow of pleasure. . . . Then I took a good look at everything I'd done . . . when I looked, I saw nothing but smoke. Smoke and spitting into the wind. There was nothing to any of it. Nothing.

Ecclesiastes 2:1–2, 10, 11 (MSG)

It hit me that what James had done in just a few weeks was actually what far too many of us do, but perhaps to a lesser and more socially acceptable degree, spread out over a longer period of time.

He decided to live selfishly, as if he were all that mattered. He would live however he felt like it at the time. The choices he made with regard to family meant he used his power and position to have multiple wives and additional "baby mommas." They meant nothing to him, the king enthroning himself at the center of his universe. He wanted everything and everyone else to spin around him. The cause of all your problems in relationships is this: "I want to be in control. I want to be God." Would you like to decide what's right and what's wrong? You say, "I don't want anyone telling me. I decide for my own life. I want to make my own rules, live my own way. If it feels good, do it." That's called playing God. You can only play at it, because you're not qualified for the role, but what it says is "I want control." To control yourself, to control other people, control your environment. That's playing God. And that's why you get out of control.

We try to control our image, what other people think of us. We don't want other people to really know what we're like, so we wear masks, pretend, fake it, and hope we make it. Deny our weaknesses and feelings.

We try to control other people. We see this in families all the time as parents try to control kids (that's impossible) and kids try to control parents (they are better at it). Wives try to control husbands; husbands try to control wives. We try to manipulate each other. We use guilt or fear or the silent treatment to control. We try to control people.

We try to control our pain. Avoid it, escape it, reduce it. By eating or not eating. By getting drunk or taking drugs or spending money or getting in relationships. "This next relationship is what I really need to feel whole."

"Oh no, that wasn't it," and you get out, and in, and out of one relationship after another. Or you develop some compulsive habit to try to control your pain.

Meanwhile God is saying, "You're not controlling anything because you need help. You need to know that I'm God and you're not." That's the cause. You have a Maker and the way you were made means that U2 was right—sometimes you can't make it on your own.

This is man's oldest problem. If you look at the start of the Bible you see that the first people, Adam and Eve, had the same problem. God put them in paradise and said, "Enjoy! Have fun! Do anything you want, except one thing—don't eat from that tree." What did they do? They made a beeline for that tree! Temptation came calling: "Eat this; you'll be the same as God." It's the basic human problem. I want to be at the center of my universe, to be God.

At various times the Bible says God wants us to love others as we love ourselves (Matt. 22:39; Eph. 5:29; 1 John 4:19–21). Most men are pretty good at loving themselves. A woman passes her reflection and tends to find something at fault with her hair or outfit. A man glimpses himself, pulls his tummy in, and thinks, "Oh yeah, baby! I've still got it!" God loves you and He is never wrong, so there's nothing wrong with loving yourself. But how good would your family say you are at loving them as much as you love yourself?

Marriage is still the bedrock of family life. The Marriage Service says it is "a gift of God in creation" and that men who consider Christian marriage are challenged to do what is most alien and foreign to our masculine nature, so we know that we need heaven's help to do it. It's a high and heroic call, to voluntarily sacrifice yourself, to put the other first. I don't know how many hundreds of weddings I have officiated, but one of the most popular readings originates from a time when men treated women as an underclass, wives as chattels, and children as inconsequential. The words the apostle Paul wrote into that culture would have stunned those who first read the manufacturer's instructions for putting together a family, and they are no less revolutionary two thousand years on:

> *Husbands, love your wives, just as Christ loved the church and gave himself up for her. . . . In this same way, husbands ought to love their wives as their own bodies. . . . After all, no one ever hated their own body, but they feed and care for their body.*
> Ephesians 5:25, 28, 29

Men know how to feed and care for themselves. If you want proof, point me to a curry. The perfectly good and natural process of self-care can show us how we should care for others too. But the way I so often fail to do that tells me something has gone wrong in the deepest part of me, which needs to be surrendered back to the one who made us, or else it will continue to twist into selfishness, insatiable greed, and hollow pride. The craving for instant gratification takes over, as men spread out a wasted life in any number of ways over years and decades. James was just doing it on fast forward with the volume turned right up. But at least he was honest about it. There are quieter and more deceptive ways to waste this life too. They can look a lot more like success than failure, until you get up close.

I don't know how many hundreds of funerals I've performed either, but one man's still haunts my memory. A rich man. I was allowed into the gated community, parked next to the Bentley he once treasured, and went to meet the undertaker at the deceased man's huge mansion (next to the home of an English Premier League striker). "He was very successful," I was told. A captain of industry. He bought and sold businesses and properties on three continents. But it became apparent that there would only be a solicitor at the funeral service, acting as executor. In the end I managed to push a few neighbors who didn't know him and one or two people from church to come along too so the church wouldn't feel so empty—I'm an extrovert!

Then I started to worry a little. Nobody wants to speak ill of the dead, and there wouldn't be many there to hear it, but what could I say at the graveside? Was he really successful? He had successfully alienated, hurt, and pushed away his former wives. The children he had no time for in this life as he buried himself in his work would now not make time even to scatter a handful of soil on his beautiful casket. It didn't appear to have been a life well lived.

At opposite ends of the spectrum, James the druggie and the successful dead man serve as two extreme examples, but there is a pattern. Whatever we may say is most important to us, whatever our good intentions, there is a temptation particularly shaped to each man that can lead to poor decisions. The decisions form a series of broad, gradual downward steps rather than a sudden clifftop drop, leading not only to separation from God, but to a relational life that ends up looking like a bad country song (by the way, all those titles at the beginning of the chapter were real attempts at chart success).

If an impartial, wise observer were to speak into the life of James, Solomon, or the Bentley owner who made a name for himself (but whose name I can't for the life of me remember), who had so much but is now only pushing up daisies, what would they say? "Stop! Turn around! Don't do it! Don't waste what's most important!" We would all say that to them.

Whatever good intentions a person says they have, it is choices and decisions that make the difference as to whether family will be something he enjoys or endures, rejoices in or regrets. On news channels and Facebook feeds, we clearly see men destroying their families, chasing skirt, success, or sales. We shake our heads and wonder how they could be so foolish: "Hey (insert name of famous bozo from today's paper), can't you see the world of pain you're heading toward? It's obvious!"

The writer of Proverbs, who many believe may have been Solomon himself, asked a rhetorical question that demands the obvious answer, "Duh!"

Can a man scoop fire into his lap without his clothes being burned?
Proverbs 6:27

Well, you should know, Solomon! Your downfall was your unrestrained desires. Can we cheat on our wives through either sex or porn? Can we make work or sport our mistress and not end up getting burned? It's obvious. Can we make more and more decisions that leave us with less and less time to spend with our children, and not end up with them saying one day that they have no time for us? It's obvious.

It's like watching Jack Bauer in *24*. I loved that show and watched the episodes back to back, but many times I would shout at the screen, "No, Jack! That's ridiculous! Oh why would you do that? Don't open that door! It's all going to blow up in your face!"

My wife would then kindly remind me, "It's not a documentary." We all know men who started out well, who you looked up to—the last guy you would ever have expected to slip up. Now they've crashed and burned. It might have all imploded within twenty-four hours. It may have been just ten minutes of madness. But for years now the shrapnel is sticking out of them and their should-have-been loved ones. Despite the best of intentions, they lost what they said was most important to them and caused irreparable damage, because of ultimately trivial pursuits.

If we were able to look on from the stands at various pivotal decision moments and see the mess they were making of their relationships and how they were screwing up their families, we would say, "It's going to end in tears! It's not worth it!"

Staying back that night for that office conversation, which led to the flirtatious remark and a lingering touch . . . if you could play the movie forward and witness the tragedy or farce it becomes, you'd rewind again and make a very different choice. It seems so obvious in other men's lives. How come we're so blind to it in our own? The little things that lead to big problems. Another piece of advice from Solomon, who was good at giving it but not at living it, was this:

> *Catch for us the foxes, the little foxes*
> *that ruin the vineyards,*
> *our vineyards that are in bloom.*
> Song of Solomon 2:15

What does that mean? Watch out for the little things that spoil the big things.

I read about how the space shuttle *Discovery* was grounded some time back, not by complex technical difficulties, but by yellow-shafted flicker woodpeckers. The little birds found the insulating foam on the shuttle's external fuel tank irresistible for pecking. Without the foam, ice forms on the tank when it is filled with the super-cold fuel—ice that can break free during liftoff and damage the giant spacecraft.

The Great Wall of China was built to preserve a family dynasty, and its twenty-two-foot-thick walls are certainly impressive, but in the end all that work didn't matter because invaders bribed the sentries and rode through the gates.

Years with tense hours sitting in airless rooms trying to hold marriages and families together have shown me that these most important of human relationships are frequently damaged not by big and obvious things such as adultery, abuse, and abandonment—but by the little things that lead that way.

Do you know the best way to bury a marriage? Lots of little digs! Criticism, lack of respect, taking each other for granted, all peck away at family cohesion and keep us from reaching the heights. Focusing on negatives develops misery. Do you try to fix what's wrong or just fix the blame?

Marcus Buckingham wrote a fascinating business book, *The One Thing You Need to Know*. What grabbed me most was not what he wrote about the workplace but about research into what it takes to have a happy marriage. The most important thing turns out to be simply focusing on the positives. Positively discriminate for your wife. Whatever happens, he says, "Find the most generous explanation for each other's behavior and believe it."[1]

Imagine how much stronger our families would be if we made a decision to slow down long enough to really see each other as people and then see the best in each other, speak the best of each other, and believe the best of each other.

"Oh," you may say, "But you don't know my situation," and it's true I never met your mother-in-law, but how bad can family get? It's a matter of perspective. Once upon a time, a man lived with his wife, two small children, and his elderly parents in a tiny hut. He tried to be patient and gracious, but the noise and crowded conditions wore him down. In desperation, he consulted the village wise man.

"Keep a cockerel in the hut too, then come see me again next week."

The next week, the man returned and told the wise elder that the living conditions were worse than ever, with all the crowing and mess in the hut. "Do you have a cow?" asked the wise elder.

The man nodded fearfully. "Take your cow into the hut as well, and come see me in a week."

Over the next several weeks, the man—on the advice of the wise elder—made room for a goat, two dogs, and all his brother's children.

Finally, he could take no more, and in a fit of anger, kicked out all the animals and guests, leaving only his wife, his children, and his parents. The home suddenly became spacious and quiet.

Thank God for your family—they are the ones God meant to live with you!

THE DYSFUNCTIONAL FAMILY OF GOD

If you want to start reading about what God thinks about family you don't have to read too far into the Bible. Genesis tells us that family was God's idea. After He had created the earth and the man, Genesis says that "God saw all that he had made, and it was very good" (1:31).

But then He saw something was not good at all. God said, "It is not good for the man to be alone. I will make a helper suitable for him" (Gen. 2:18). Notice, here's the prototype man, in the perfect environment, with the perfect job—if you're the outdoor type—and the perfect boss. He's at the head of the food chain, the top of the tree (couldn't resist that one).

But God said, "It is not good for the man to be alone."

That's still true whether you're a married or single man. You were made for relationship. It's a basic need like air, water, and pizza. We need relationships. Man was not made to be alone, so God created the first human family. He addressed Adam's aloneness and met that need for companionship. He made Eve, and when he saw her standing there, Adam said, "Whoa—man!", which is where the word "babe" comes from in Hebrew. It was the first marriage. But were they the "perfect couple"?

It's surprising how often you'll hear in wedding speeches some reference to "the perfect couple." There's no such thing.

Even that first family proved to be dysfunctional. I related earlier how in their desire to be like God and be in control, Adam and Eve fell into temptation then fell out with each other—blaming each other, a reptile, and even God for their problems. Theologians call this first sin the fall. One of their kids kills the other on the way home from church, and family goes downhill from there.

But do you know what the great news is? God never gave up on the family. Running alongside all of their stories, from one problem family to the next, is God himself. Sticking close, working out a plan, with a purpose that always prevails.

God is a dad. He knows every family, every relationship, has its ups and downs. He's not in denial even if we are. He is unchanging in His promise, power, and perfect love. Like any good father, at times God has to discipline His children to be kind. Often they are at a loss to understand everything He's doing. But when you flick through the pages of God's big family album, the story consistently portrayed is that even when God's people are unfaithful, He is always faithful. While they deserve nothing, He provides, protects, and blesses. When they don't stay loving, He never stops. They feud, He forgives. When they're weak, He gives them His strength.

I love to sit and look through old family albums. I think it will be a shame when they're all just on the cloud and we don't get to turn page after page of memories of laughter, occasions, holidays, people, and places. I'm amazed at how the kids and my waistline have grown so fast. I'm amazed how I thought I looked cool. Some people reading this will never have known of the time when you excitedly waited for the roll of film used that week in Spain to come back from the chemist, only to find your thumb in the picture instead of Grandad's head.

Like you, we generally only got the camera out on happy days. Before selfies took over, we'd put our arms around each other and say "cheese!" So every day in the book looks like the best day of our lives. Our family album can't possibly tell the full story. The mistakes are just deleted. But when you go through God's family album, it's different. You'll see that while there are some glorious shots and awesome landscapes, the portraits are not always too flattering. He isn't ashamed to show us the truth about His family—warts and all—because it's the only one He's got and they all have lessons to teach us for our own families.

Turn a page—there smiles Abraham, who tells lies about his wife but ends up being called the father of faith.

God doesn't alter Noah's red eyes or not tell us about the flash that embarrassed his sons when he had a few too many to celebrate his ark landing safely.

Flick over to Moses the murderer, Samson the weak strongman, David the adulterer king, Rahab the prostitute. Page after page of broken people, fractured families. Nobody's left out or stood at the back behind a big hat. The Bible holds the unenhanced, unaltered photos of needy, greedy, weedy, seedy people. God's family. They get listed in Hebrews chapter 11, where God's title caption declares that He is "not ashamed to be called their God" (v. 16).

Now turn another page. No, a few more. Go back. Stop.

A picture of a baby. Amazing!

God has stepped out of heaven and right into the picture. The infinite infant! Is this the perfect family? He's not in a palace but a feeding trough. In the next shot He's comforted at the breast of one who is nearly a single mum. A jealous king wants to kill Him. His parents lose Him for a few days. His cousin eats locusts for lunch while His brothers and sisters stand around calling Him crazy.

Not a perfect picture, is it? Dr. Martyn Lloyd-Jones said the Bible is the most honest book in the world. Why? Because God tells it like it is.

Families come in all kinds of shapes and sizes, but God knows it is not good to be alone, so in His perfect love He gave us this imperfect gift. It's not too late for you to make the changes you need to make in your family.

God says the church is family too, which means we shouldn't be surprised if it has its share of strange and annoying people we'd rather not bother with. Love them anyway. Loving people who are different is the way God makes our hearts grow bigger. It's not too late for you to try to connect or reconnect to a spiritual family.

It's too late for the successful man whose name I'd only remember if I went and looked at the gravestone. The time to make the decisions and changes in our schedules that reflect a shift in our priorities is today.

It's not too late for James, I'm glad to say. I was swinging between praying for him and despairing of him, but I admit I was shocked when he knocked on my door again recently and said he wanted to go on our 12-Step Recovery Course, which helps hundreds of people overcome their hurts, habits, and hang-ups. He looked like Gollum on a crash diet, but I saw a glimpse of the man he could be again glint through a newfound determination born out of despair: "I want to give up crack, gambling, smoking; I want to live, Anthony." He had come to the point of knowing "I can't help myself," and that's where you find the help you need has a name—Jesus Christ.

Where there's hope, there is life—and vice versa. If he sees this through, there's hope for transformation, which may be the first step to some reconciliation in his world.

It's not too late for you. Whatever your relational past, present, or future, you have a heavenly Father from whom every earthly family derives its name. He has the full picture. He sees the generations before that led to you being born and alive now. He holds plans full of hope and a bright future in His hands. God knows there are nuts in every family tree. He knows families can be great or a great pain—no family is perfect. Not yours. Not His. He can work with that; He specializes in it.

So smile.

Smile!

Wider! Say "cheese!"

Why?

He wants you and yours in His family album.

Chapter 5

Failure

"I've missed more than 9,000 shots in my career. I've lost almost 300 games. Twenty-six times, I've been trusted to take the game-winning shot and missed. I've failed over and over and over again in my life. And that is why I succeed."

– MICHAEL JORDAN

A COUPLE IN THEIR SIXTIES were celebrating their thirtieth wedding anniversary when God said to them, "You guys have done so well, I'm so pleased, whatever you pray today will be answered."

"I'd love a round-the-world cruise," she said—and bam! The tickets appeared in her hand.

The guy looked sheepish then declared, "Well, really, I'd like to be married to someone thirty years younger."

Bam! He's ninety!

That's what you call a FAIL.

I love watching fail videos. Seeing people crashing off skateboards, motorbikes, and water skis, preferably into the person holding the camera.

As I write, our national team has just crashed out of a major tournament. We idolize success and train so it seems we can't lose, but then people fail. Every day we witness the greater and more permanent failures of politicians, movie stars, and sporting heroes. Closer to home, friends let us down, business partnerships fold, husbands fail wives, parents fail their kids, and kids fail to live up to the expectations of their parents.

We try. Try again. Fail again. Everybody fails. It is a great universal truth: nobody's perfect. Even successful people fail. In fact, successful people fail *more* because they try more things more often, and have to learn from their failures.

We will all fail often. It's not as if we fail once and say, "I've learned now and will never fail again." It isn't a question of how can we never fail again; we will all fail and keep on failing—until death stops us. Anyone close to me knows I have my failings, but I do not let my failings have me, so they do not make me a failure.

The big question then is how can we fail successfully? How do imperfect people improve? How do we learn to move from saying, "I am a failure" to the more correct and healthy, "I have failed"? Because failure is an event, not a person.

I talk to too many people wrestled to the ground by the weight of failure—pinned to the mat by their fear of failing again—so they give up fighting and stop trying.

Fear of failure can cause us to be indecisive. We can't make decisions or act on them; afraid we're going to make the wrong move again, we don't move forward.

Fear of failure can make you a workaholic, because it might all come crashing down any minute.

Fear of failure can make you a perfectionist. It's never quite right, you see; you're never satisfied.

Nobody wants to fail. But some will do anything to win—lower their moral standards, try to cover up, blame someone else, or hurt people to hide their failures. Is there any way for us *not* to fear failure while not denying the consequences? How do we relate to a perfect God? Could there be a way for imperfect people who break relationship with a holy God by breaking His commandments and heart to come back to Him who embodies perfection?

From beginning to end the Bible's family history shows how that way has been made. I'm glad I'm not in the Bible because everyone's failures are all on show. But every page also tells us our failure is not final. Proverbs 24:16 says, "For though the righteous fall seven times, they rise again," so even the best stumble at times. People trying their best to do what's right sometimes get it wrong. Successful people are not people who never fail! I'd much rather have someone work for me who tried heroically and failed spectacularly than a mediocre play-safe who never even ran for first base.

The apostle Paul is a great example of this: "We are hard pressed on every side, but not crushed; perplexed, but not in despair . . . struck down, but not destroyed" (2 Cor. 4:8–9). In other words, it's not over till it's over, and it's not over yet because you're still breathing.

The 1981 film *Chariots of Fire* told the true story of athlete Eric Liddell, known as the "Flying Scotsman," who went on to become a missionary in China. He refused to run on Sundays, so he had to withdraw from the 100 meter race, his best event. Instead, he entered the 400 meter. As he went to the starting blocks, an American masseur slipped a piece of paper into Liddell's hand with a quotation from 1 Samuel 2:30 (ESV), which reads: "Those who honor me I will honor." Liddell ran with that piece of paper in his hand and not only won the race but broke the world record.

A scene earlier in the film inspires me most. Liddell ran in an event that saw athletes from England, Ireland, and Scotland compete against each other. When the gun sounded, there was a lot of shoving for the inside lane. He collided with J. J. Gillies of England

and fell. He sat dazed for a moment, not knowing whether he could get up. An official screamed, "Get up and run!"

Liddell jumped to his feet and in his unorthodox style took off after the pack, which was about twenty yards ahead of him. In a race that's over a quarter of a mile long that's a huge distance to make up. With forty yards to go, he was back in third place, then second. Right at the tape he pulled his head back and stuck his chest out, which is when he said he most keenly felt the pleasure of God. Liddell passed Gillies and won—then collapsed in total exhaustion. Medics had to carry him off the track.

An article appeared the next day in the *Scotsman*:

> The circumstances in which Liddell won the race made it a performance bordering on the miraculous. Veterans whose memories take them back thirty-five years and in some cases longer in the history of athletics were unanimous in the opinion that Liddell's win in the quarter mile was the greatest track performance they had ever seen.[1]

Why was it so great? The trophy has been melted down and the fixture would have been long forgotten by now, except there's something glorious about getting up after you've been knocked down. Remember Rocky? If you don't stay down, you're a winner.

Theodore Roosevelt summed it up in his speech at the Sorbonne:

> It is not the critic who counts; not the man who points out how the strong man stumbles, or where the doer of deeds could have done them better. The credit belongs to the man who is actually in the arena, whose face is marred by dust and sweat and blood; who strives valiantly; who errs, who comes short again and again, because there is no effort without error and shortcoming; but who does actually strive to

do the deeds; who knows the great enthusiasms, the great devotions; who spends himself in a worthy cause; who at the best knows in the end the triumph of high achievement, and who at the worst, if he fails, at least fails while daring greatly, so that his place shall never be with those cold and timid souls who neither know victory nor defeat.[2]

Everybody stumbles in the race of life, but not everyone gets up again—what will you do? Failure is going to remain a part of the rest of your life. It's normal, part of being human. The Bible says, "All have sinned and fall short of the glory of God" (Rom. 3:23). Now, of course, not all failure is a result of sin, but the Greek word for sin used there literally means to have "missed the mark—so as not to gain the prize." The English word *sin* was coined from an archery term referring to an arrow that doesn't hit or barely miss the target but one that doesn't even have the range to get close enough to scare it. A pastor preaching on this verse said, "Thank God, He forgives our falling shorts!"

It's true! We all have falling shorts and short fallings!

I teach a course for people investigating whether or not Christianity might help make better sense of their story, called My Life Workshop. The first session looks backwards at our lives, segmenting them through the years while looking at the positives and negatives and how together they shape our lives, like two sides of the same coin. Later we look at our lives like a book and give various parts of our story chapter headings. It's a time of tears and smiles for many. Mapping out our lives like this means we put on paper the ups and downs of our own stories and share as much as we are comfortable with of the ups and downs. Nobody ever has all "ups"—mine looks like an ECG printout, but at least my heart's still beating so there's hope.

If ever there was a man with ups and downs it was one of Jesus' closest friends, the apostle Simon Peter. Peter was one of the most successful failures in Scripture. My heart warms to him every time I see his name in the Bible because he will either be riding high on the crest of a wave or plummeting to ground zero without a parachute. I'm sure you will resonate with his life story too.

An old bus driver and a preacher both died and stood at heaven's gate and St. Peter came out. The bus driver obviously had terrible eyesight as he had to be led by his hand to a huge palatial mansion. The preacher was then shown a little shed out the back.

"Hang on, your Saintship," said the preacher. "He's just a bus driver! What about all those sermons I preached through the years?"

"When you preached, people slept," St. Peter explained. "When he drove his bus, people prayed."

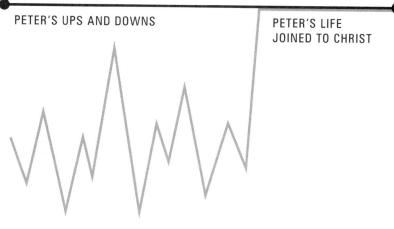

JESUS' PERFECT OBEDIENCE

PETER'S UPS AND DOWNS

PETER'S LIFE
JOINED TO CHRIST

Yes, Peter is the guy in lots of corny jokes, holding the keys to the gates of heaven, asking difficult questions, and giving out mansions or sheds dependent on the answers. But if you track what we know about him from the Gospels and history, you'd see that he'd be the last person to go for a performance-based celestial entry plan. He would tell you about how his journey of ups and downs somehow led to that elevated position, a true story of success and failure since he was a man always jumping in with both feet and landing in trouble.

UP

We don't know how long Peter had known Jesus, but the chances are he would at least have heard of Him because they were from the same region. His new life as a Jesus follower got started the same as anyone else's, including yours and mine, when he said yes to the simple call, "*Follow Me!*" (see Luke 5:1–8). He was called from his fishing business to catch six-footers, to become lead fisher of men, first among equals of the initial band of followers that would spearhead the movement others called "the way."

Jesus nicknamed him "Rocky" (the name "Peter" means "rock"), determined to draw out Peter's potential by making him leader of the twelve men Jesus called to be with Him and represent Him as apostles. From now on Peter would be the first follower, and his floundering following is a boom-and-bust pattern for the rest of us.

DOWN

Peter's pattern of thinking is characterized by the phrase "I know best." He allowed Jesus into his boat so he could listen to His sermon, but complained when this landlubber carpenter started to give him fishing advice on where to put his net out. There was just enough diamond there in the rough for him to eventually say just what Jesus was looking for, a good acronym to remember: BYSSIW.

"Because you say so, I will" (Luke 5:5).

When Peter finally did as he was told, he got more fish in five minutes than he'd seen in as many months. His reaction? "Go away from me, Lord; I am a sinful man!" (Luke 5:8). A very appropriate response! I can't draw on a chart a line high enough above Peter's up-and-down life to represent the gulf between it and the consistent, holy, beautiful, powerful perfection of God that he caught a glimpse of that day in Jesus Christ. Isaiah 55:9 simply tells us, "As the heavens are higher than the earth, so are my ways higher than your ways." So how can an imperfect, sinful man relate to God? Keep watching.

UP

Quite the fisherman's tale. One to tell the grandkids. How one stormy night, *just like Jesus*, Peter walked on water (Matt. 14:25–31). He said to Jesus, "Lord, if it's you, . . . tell me to come to you on the water" (v. 28) because it was his job to follow first. Against all common sense and natural danger signals, this uncommon yet ordinary man stepped out—to do the impossible. Guess what—he did it! Only a couple of baby steps, but if you think that's easy, invite me to watch you try. What Jesus wants from His followers is that we take a step at a time, to become like Him. Why wait till the end of the book to get your feet wet? What have you got to lose? And if it is true you gain everything. Ask Him now, "If You are real, make Yourself real to me." Peter actually walked on water, just like Jesus. What an "up" that must have been!

DOWN

Splash! Peter took his eyes off Jesus and put them on his circumstances and his heart gave way to fear. The Bible says we walk by faith, not by sight, but Peter didn't follow perfectly. He was impetuous, often overconfident. After the spiritual high came a dunking, with Jesus having to pull him out. That's a great picture of what happened in his life again and again! He'd be sunk, without Jesus.

UP

Peter was the first to recognize and say who Jesus really was (Matt. 16:15–17)! The talk of the town was a debate about who Jesus was— so He asked His disciples, "Who do you say I am?"

Peter spoke up, "You are the Messiah, the Son of the living God" (v. 16). Jesus commended him for that insight and said that God the Father had revealed it to him. Then He said that this declaration, knowing Jesus is God, is the key of the kingdom.

Seeing and saying who Jesus really is, whatever anyone else might say, opens the gates of heaven. Knowing Christ opens the door and makes all the difference for any imperfect person. What would your answer be? Who is Jesus? I say He is the Christ, and I'm betting my life I am right!

If you get this question right, you are given a full pardon and power to live a new life despite whatever you got wrong, despite the failures, mistakes, and sins that should exclude you from God because they fall so short of His glory. Peter only had a glimpse, but he was the first to see and say who Jesus is, and Jesus said that he was holding the keys to open up heaven. It doesn't get much better than that.

DOWN

Read on just a couple of verses. Peter opens his mouth and puts his foot in it, presuming to tell the same person he just admitted is God what He should and shouldn't do, and ends up being likened to Satan as a result (Matt. 16:21–23). Why? Because he is trying to put a stumbling block in the way of God's plans. When God says you're aiding and abetting the enemy? That's a fail!

UP

The last supper. In Matthew 26:33, Peter promises to stick with Jesus to the end—no matter what, no bother, 100 percent.

> *I'm better than all the rest of these guys—I love You most,*
> *You can always rely on me Jesus,*
> *I'm Your best pal,*
> *I'll never let You down.*

DOWN

#Fail! As Jesus knew and predicted ahead of time, the rooster crowed when Peter chickened out. His failure is one of the worst betrayals in history: he sells out and denies even knowing Jesus three times, to save his own skin (Matt. 26:69–75). Standing by a fire, three different audiences ask, "Do you know Him?"

"I don't know Him!" Oh, but you do know Him—surely . . .

"Nah, never heard of the guy!"

Do you know Him? Didn't I see you with Him?

"You're talking crap! Listen—I don't freaking know Him!"

It doesn't get much lower than that. And Jesus looked right at him as He was taken to the cross, where His friend Peter was nowhere to be seen.

UP

But the cross was not the end of Jesus' story, or Peter's! You can't keep a God-man down, and after a couple of days people started saying they had met with Jesus again. He was resurrected from the dead. He appeared to one woman, and some women, and again to a pair on their way from Jerusalem to the village of Emmaus. Eventually He popped up in all kinds of places where He appeared in many convincing ways to hundreds of them.

But there was one man He really wanted a word with. Jesus kept saying He wanted to meet personally and particularly with Peter.

Peter had failed, so he went back to what he used to be pretty good at, fishing. Actually, Jesus was always better than him at it, and one day a mysterious stranger appeared on the shore to once again tell Peter how to have a net-bursting catch. Jesus cooked some of the catch for them before taking Peter for a long walk on the beach.

John 21:15–23 records beautifully how Peter heard that his failures were never going to have the final word. He had denied Jesus three times, so now, standing by another fire with Jesus looking at him again, three times Peter is asked, "Do you love Me most?"

Peter kicks the sand. "You know I admire You, but I messed up . . ."

"Do you love Me?"

"You know, but . . ."

"Are you going to try to love Me again?"

Oh, really? Yes please.

Peter doesn't even get full marks in this test, but Jesus says, "I want you to lead again, to love and look after My people." There are no perfect followers, and Jesus limits Himself to work with what's available. My specialty is teaching on leadership, and I have discovered that the very best human leaders are all too aware of their own fragility, and of the fragility of those they lead.

A leader of a large company found out one of his trainees just lost them a £10,000 deal and called him in.

"Are you going to sack me?" the trainee asked.

"Sack you?! No way! I just spent £10,000 training you!"

I love how the conversation ended—Peter started to compare himself with some other guy and Jesus said, "What's he got to do with you?" Then His final words were the very same words it all started with years before: "*Follow Me!*"

There's a great word the Bible uses for how God forgives us when we inevitably fail, and it's "justified." Someone said that means it's "just as if I'd never sinned." Jesus makes it possible that now it's just as if none of what had happened, ever happened. Not just a clean slate, a brand-new iPad!

Peter is outrageously loved and totally restored for the task ahead, Jesus is going to return to His heavenly Father, and He's giving Peter another go. None of Peter's failures had taken Him by surprise; after all, He predicted them in advance! Great stuff.

Maybe the ups and downs were over?

UP

Jesus told His friends, "I'll never leave you," but then He seemed to as He ascended to heaven. After a very long prayer meeting, the Spirit of Jesus came back to earth and then Peter, who had been a chicken when Jesus was crucified, stands up in the same city where it happened, Jerusalem, and preaches a lion-hearted sermon. Three thousand people responded, which as a preacher myself I would say is not bad for a beginner.

DOWN

In that sermon, Peter quoted a passage from the Old Testament that promised that the Holy Spirit would now be poured out on all flesh—all people (Acts 2:17). But contrary to Jesus' final instructions to go into the whole world and tell everyone about Him, Peter went nowhere. He certainly didn't want to go to the Gentiles, to non-Jewish people.

UP

It took a dramatic vision—repeated three times; we are seeing a pattern here—where God told Peter nobody's unclean and Jesus makes everyone kosher to get Peter to cross the doorstep of a Roman soldier named Cornelius and tell him about Jesus' life, death, resurrection, and message. Peter became the first apostle to reach out to non-Jewish people when he went to Cornelius's house, and everyone who heard became Christ followers too.

DOWN

In Acts chapter 15, Peter said he knew God chose him to be the one to reach out to Gentiles, but that doesn't mean he liked it. It ends up that Jesus calls and sends Paul, not Peter, to become the apostle to the Gentiles. Could prejudice have held Peter back from a part of his destiny?

So, you get to the gates of heaven and Peter is there with the keys like in the cartoons. You might want to ask Peter, "How do imperfect people get in?"

How do imperfect, up-and-down people enter the kingdom of God and relate to a God who is absolutely consistent—holy, holy, holy?

How do we get in through the gates of heaven, Peter? How do people who fail, whose only true consistency is to fail consistently— earthly creatures so up and down and far away even in our highest "ups" from God's perfect standards—how can we connect intimately now and forever to such an awesome, majestic, perfect God as the Bible describes? How can failures be saved? How can you and I be "perfect failures"?

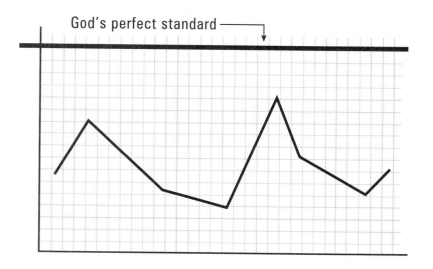

God's perfect standard

Acts 15 finds Barnabas and Paul in a place called Antioch. Predominately it was non-Jewish people who were finding their way back to God and becoming Christ followers simply by putting their faith in the message the apostles preached, what Jesus had accomplished for them through the cross and the empty tomb. But a group from a Jewish background turned up and began to teach that this was too easy, and not enough. If they want to be real Christians, these Jews argued, they have to follow the customs of Moses, obey the dietary laws, and so on.

Actually, the "so on" bit is painful; it's, *ahem*, circumcision. The men have to fully behave like orthodox Jews to be acceptable to God—and He's checking in your pants.

But circumcision started out as a sign of a promise God made, not a performance for men to keep. Throughout the Old Testament there are signs of God's perfect promise to bless and do good to imperfect people. To Adam and Eve, it was the clothes they wore that covered them at the cost of a sacrifice. To Cain, it was a sign that marked him out for protection and not punishment, despite his being the first murderer. To Noah, the sign accompanying the promise was a rainbow.

God appeared to a very old, childless Babylonian named Abram (later renamed Abraham) and promised to bless him *and* his millions of descendants if he followed God. They entered into a covenant, and as a sign of that promise a sacrifice was made while Abraham slept—to show that God will do by faith what Abraham could never do by trying.

Centuries later, the Law was given to Moses, and God promised to be with him and bless the nation if they obeyed it. The infiltrators in Antioch said that the sign of that agreement was circumcision (I'm sure Moses would have preferred a rainbow), but actually circumcision started way before Moses and the commandments. It was given as a sign to Abraham, who gets the title "the father of faith" because he just believed God, and God said, "That's what I was looking for."

Because of that basic misunderstanding, these men came with a "Jesus AND" plan to instruct the new non-Jewish disciples. They came carrying sharp implements, a calendar of special days to observe, and a shopping list of what to eat and not eat.

The way to be saved now, they explained, is to follow the example of Jesus—who was an observant and circumcised Jew—and follow all the laws, customs, and commands of Jewish people. In other words, you're not really a Christian unless you are Jewish first. You have to be a Jew and follow Jesus. That's the "Jesus AND" plan. It plagued the church from the earliest times, and much of the rest of the New Testament addresses and opposes it, but it is still with us today in various self-denying, self-exalting guises.

The leaders in Antioch, Paul and Barnabas, ended up in sharp conflict with these teachers. "No! These men don't need to try to keep the Law of Moses and be circumcised—there is no 'Jesus AND' plan. There's only the Jesus plan! All or nothing!"

There's no way the two groups could compromise on this because they were bringing directly opposing messages, so they decided, "Let's get this settled once and for all—we'll go to the guys like Peter who first knew Jesus and walked with Him in Galilee and get a firsthand opinion. We'll get a ruling from the apostles."

So they met for a historic meeting, where they outlined to the apostles and church leaders in Jerusalem how everywhere the gospel is spreading, people who are not Jews are believing it. They even brought one named Titus along to show this was not a hypothetical question. What do we do with someone like him?

Some from the legalistic faction with a Pharisaic background answered in a way that would bring tears to Titus's eyes: "Circumcise him, so he can follow Jesus AND try to be a perfect Jew from now on" (see Acts 15:5).

Then all eyes turn as a perfect failure stood to speak. They call him by his Hebrew name, Simon, here. Remember, Peter had been brought up as a Law-observing Jew. He'd been circumcised. He wanted to answer the monumental question once and for all—not just the history and future of the church but eternities hung in the balance. You can hear the frustration in his words, because as he looked at his own track record, he knew we have all failed and will fail.

At Police Training School, I was taught lifesaving by an ex-SBS legend whose method was literally sink or swim. Hapless new recruits either floated and started to doggy paddle or became an object of the lesson. Ernie's number one rule was that you can't save anyone who is still trying to save himself.

Reflecting on all the ups and downs of his life, Peter saw that he couldn't save himself now any more than he could when he tried to walk on water. The only one who had been consistent and perfect in his story was Jesus—from the day he first heard Jesus say by the lake, "Follow Me," till he heard Him say it on the beach again.

Brothers, you know that some time ago God made a choice among you that the Gentiles might hear from my lips the message of the gospel and believe. God, who knows the heart, showed that he accepted them by giving the Holy Spirit to them, just as he did to us. He did not discriminate between us and them, for he purified their hearts by faith. Now then, why do you try to test God by putting on the necks of Gentiles a yoke that neither we nor our ancestors have been able to bear? No! We believe it is through the grace of our Lord Jesus that we are saved, just as they are.

Acts 15:7–11

This is amazing! Peter said race doesn't matter; it doesn't matter to God where we're from or what our background is. What matters is Jesus—just Jesus. Believing in Him changes our past, our future—everything. Because of Christ, because of God's grace, God doesn't give us what we deserve but what we need. He accepts us and makes us acceptable. We don't need more rituals or sacrifices; He makes us the temple He wants to live in now by His Holy Spirit.

Peter concluded that it's futile to keep trying to do for ourselves by religious effort what Jesus came to undo because it never worked. We are never going to live "UP" to that. We can't live up to God's standards of perfection. We need His grace to come down to us.

There is no "Jesus AND"—it's just Jesus. That's the grace plan. Look at the illustration on the next page. God's perfect antidote to our imperfections and failures is grace. The grace of Jesus still comes to perfect perfect failures. (You may need to read that twice to get it.)

Jesus is saying "Follow Me" and from the day we say yes to that, we connect, by grace, to His perfection.

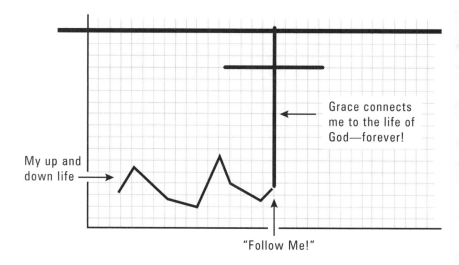

My up and down life →

Grace connects me to the life of God—forever!

"Follow Me!"

We can't raise ourselves to heaven's standard any more than you could build a ladder and climb up it to reach the sun. We stop trying to save ourselves when we discover it's not "Jesus and" but Jesus only! Jesus Christ was the only perfect man. The only sinless one—the only one qualified to save us, and He has done it all on the cross.

Nobody's perfect. If I handed in the test paper of my life in the perfection examination, I'd get a FAIL! But someone else did the test for me. His perfect obedience, sacrifice on the cross, and resurrection mean Jesus got the A+, 100 percent—absolute perfection. Keep on reading as I explain more about how just when we need it most, He says, "You can have My result, swap My perfection for your imperfection." This is the offer God extends to every one of us today—have you accepted it? It's a great swap.

What a difference it makes to live knowing you are perfectly forgiven, that you've already got a pass with flying colors! Years later, Peter, the *perfected* failure, wrote a letter to Christians scattered and persecuted in many nations where he explains in one line how the trade works: "For Christ also suffered once for sins, the righteous for the unrighteous, to bring you to God" (1 Peter 3:18).

From the point in my life where I own up to my imperfections and come back to God, I receive Christ's perfection, not just as a onetime deal—it's forever and ever! I die to myself so I can live for Him. The Bible says it's like I am now taken out of my earthly and time-limited life to be seated in heaven with Him (Eph. 2:6). I have a totally different perspective: I reign in life because I live in a new kingdom (Rom. 5:17); I have been taken out of the old one to live a new life as a new creation (2 Cor. 5:17). Look again at that diagram opposite and you'll see what I mean.

Maybe you have never had anyone love you unconditionally. Well, you do now. The only absolutely consistent love and faithfulness and perfection in Peter's life was Jesus. Jesus said, "Follow Me," and the two connected. When we do that, nothing can separate us from the love of God that is in Christ Jesus! Whenever Peter was out of his depth, Jesus reached in and pulled him up, out, and back to Himself.

Whenever, however, wherever we blow it—Jesus wants us back! He came looking for Peter just as God came looking for Adam in the garden, and He comes looking for us too, not to punish us but because we matter to Him—and because He has a job, a purpose, for us. No matter how badly you feel you have blown it. No matter how deep the hole you have dug for yourself, it's no accident you are reading this book right now. Jesus has come looking to restore you and give you a reason not just to exist—but to live! He walks right into the heartbreak and mess with the irrational invitation to try again, His way, in His power!

It's not, "Never fail so you can follow Me."

It's love that never fails, saying, "Follow Me! With all your ups and downs." Like a teacher at the beginning of term who says, "You already got an A; now that the pressure is off, let's have some fun and start learning together."

I try and fail and pick up and start again because I'm on the grace plan. I already got an A! The most important A ever: ACCEPTANCE. Acceptance from God! He overlooks my failures because He sees my future—as His perfected son! How? By grace! (If you accept His grace today, He will accept you forever!)

THERE BUT FOR THE GRACE OF GOD . . .

If you search Anthony Delaney online, you may find I "own the page" because my name comes up a lot in the searches as a result of my writing, blogs, and so on. But on the image page there are links to a homeless namesake, the same age as me, who was discovered living rough at Gatwick Airport for months.

That old saying came to mind when I read Mr. Delaney's sad story and wondered what kind of train wreck I would have made of my life if I were still in the driver's seat. If Jesus hadn't pulled me up and called me to follow Him:

There but for the grace of God go I.

That phrase is credited to my fellow Mancunian, sixteenth-century Protestant reformer John Bradford, who was imprisoned for his faith for many years in the Tower of London. Whenever he saw a criminal going to be hanged for his crimes, he would say, "There but for the grace of God goes John Bradford."

Bradford himself was eventually burned at Smithfield. He had been shown in a dream the night before that this would happen. He kissed the wood and the stake before lifting his eyes to heaven, then told the man dying alongside him, "Be of good comfort, brother, for we shall have a merry supper with the Lord this night." He knew the love that never fails—the grace of God really is amazing.

We who have failed and will fail again can kiss the cross because it is there we connect to perfection—by grace. Peter knew failure, but he knew something greater: that while he was going under for at least the third time, a nail-pierced hand had reached down so that by grace he has been saved, is being saved, and will be saved forever.

Chapter 6

Friends

The Thousandth Man

One man in a thousand, Solomon says,
Will stick more close than a brother.
And it's worthwhile seeking him half your days
If you find him before the other.

Nine hundred and ninety-nine depend
On what the world sees in you,
But the Thousandth Man will stand your friend
With the whole round world agin you.

'Tis neither promise nor prayer nor show
Will settle the finding for 'ee.
Nine hundred and ninety-nine of 'em go
By your looks, or your acts, or your glory.

But if he finds you and you find him,
The rest of the world don't matter;

For the Thousandth Man will sink or swim
With you in any water.

You can use his purse with no more talk
Than he uses yours for his spendings,
And laugh and meet in your daily walk
As though there had been no lendings.

Nine hundred and ninety-nine of 'em call
For silver and gold in their dealings;
But the Thousandth Man he's worth 'em all
Because you can show him your feelings.

His wrong's your wrong, and his right's your right,
In season or out of season.
Stand up and back it in all men's sight
With that for your only reason!

Nine hundred and ninety-nine can't bide
The shame or mocking or laughter,
But the Thousandth Man will stand by your side
To the gallows-foot—and after!

– RUDYARD KIPLING

"I . . . treat the Lord Jesus Christ as a personal friend. His is not a creed, a mere empty doctrine; but it is he himself we have."

– D. L. MOODY

Who's your best friend?

At primary school I had a best friend. I don't know when Paul became my best friend, but it happened well before he turned to me one day and asked that childish question that either breaks it or cements it for sure—the earliest DTR ("define the relationship") point where, as a kid, you turn to someone and ask, "Who's your best friend?"

Depending on the response, hoping no other name gets

mentioned, you can ask, "Am I your best friend?" or you can put it right out there: "Will you be my best friend?"

There is a choice and a risk with every word and breath. Even at this stage the other may say, "No, I don't want to be your best friend." But to hear "okay" is definitely worth the risk.

Paul Marshall was officially my best friend from the age of seven through ten. Even though he was posh. I knew he was posh because his mum and dad had a car. He was smaller than me, with a shock of blond hair. We laughed all the time. We were deadly kung fu superheroes in the playground, while in class we drew superhero cartoons. He was great at art and I was good with words so we *knew* one day we'd have our own version of DC or Marvel comics, "MarDel"!

But six months before the end of primary school, Paul told me his parents were moving and he would be living a long, long way away. (I now realize it wasn't that far, but your world is tiny when you're a kid.) My family didn't own a car. We didn't have a phone. We said we'd write and that nothing would stop the comic dream. He gave me his phone number. As I said, they were posh.

We wrote a few times about the comics. One day I walked to the call box down the road and put my money in. A very posh boy came on the other end of the line. I couldn't speak a word to him and just put the receiver down.

That's the sad tale of how I lost my first best friend. You might be heartless enough to not be too moved by it, in which case I don't want you to be my friend, but years later when I was in a counseling course looking at grief, we were given a list of bereavement symptoms and asked to look back on our lives and think when we first felt grief. The name Paul Marshall surfaced immediately. I realized right then that I spent my high school years looking for a smaller, blond friend, preferably called Paul, to replace the one I'd lost.

Making friends makes you vulnerable.

The offer of friendship and the chance of being rejected go hand in hand. Friendships change, people come and go. Once you have a friend, they might leave you or you could fall out over something. It could spill over from the individual to a whole group.

We experience hurt after losing friends and may end up isolating ourselves, because we have insulated ourselves. A crust forms around our heart. "It's probably better not to put my heart out there in case I get hurt again." But adding loneliness to your lot only compounds the problem. As John Donne wrote, "No man is an island, entire of itself."

BILLY NO-MATES

I just went out for a meal by myself. My wife, Zoe, is at work today. I am only just an extrovert, so at times I like to do that anyway. The secret is to take a book with you so you don't look like a loner. The truth is, I am never a loner, because I am never alone. You may think this sounds odd, but I also carry on a mental conversation with Jesus over a meal like that, because He's promised never to leave me alone.

When God made the prototype man, Adam, and put him in the perfect environment, with fulfilling work and the best boss, He noted: "It is not good for the man to be alone" (Gen. 2:18).

It's really not good, and we're alone too much. Even when we're with people.

Most men haven't got many friends, not really good friends. I observe that women are usually much better at this than men, because to be a friend you need to be a good listener and think about the other person's needs, not just your own! A study by linguistics professor Deborah Tannen said that in conversation women do "Rapport-talk"—where listening is actually waiting for the other person to finish so you have heard what they said, while men do "Report-talk," listening just enough for a gap to open so you can say what you want to say.[1] Women in my experience tend to be better than men at such "soft" skills as genuine rapport building, which are actually just good manners. A friend of mine, who heads a recovery group for people with life-controlling issues, often advises them, "Take the cotton wool out of your ears and put it in your mouth."

Proverbs 18:24 advises that if you want to have many friends, you have to show yourself to be friendly. How? Friendly people are other-focused. Take the microphone away from your own mouth and put it on the other person.

I love the story from the nineteenth century about a woman who had the rare opportunity to dine with the two most famous living Englishmen of her day: Prime Ministers William Gladstone and Benjamin Disraeli. Who impressed her more? She said, "When I went to lunch with William Gladstone I was convinced that I was dining with the greatest living Englishman. But when I went to lunch with Disraeli, I was convinced that he was dining with the greatest living Englishwoman!"

I shudder to think how many times I've missed out on the possibility of making friends because I was too busy making an impression, or not even fully present because I was busy reading what my Facebook "friends" had to say—the temptation has never been stronger than in the digital age to gather more superficial relationships instead of developing real friendships.

For a long time in my life, I was quite happy just to be intimate with my wife and superficial with everyone else. Where did that come from? Well, as a police officer I only had buddies who were other officers, and some of those relationships, forged in tough circumstances, remain strong and deep today. A fellow ex-officer who I haven't worked with in decades only yesterday reminded me, "We always stand together." That was true. I had serious trust issues with other people, but old King Harry got it right about how scars won together bind a band:

And Crispin Crispian shall ne'er go by,
From this day to the ending of the world,
But we in it shall be remembered;
We few, we happy few, we band of brothers;
For he to-day that sheds his blood with me
Shall be my brother; be he ne'er so vile.
William Shakespeare, *Henry V* (Act 4, Scene 3)

Maybe you can look back on a time when you were part of a band of brothers. If so, you're a blessed man, and rarer still if that remains the case today. Superficiality is the norm. Many men greet each other with, "How's it going?" and a slap on the back but don't really expect, much less *want*, an answer. Body language experts tell us the number of slaps on the back in a man hug increases proportionately in relation to how uncomfortable we are and the more quickly we want to get away. For fun, one of my pals has perfected what he calls the "awkward hug," where you don't put your head to either side as one would expect but just keep your head very straight—and watch what the other, very embarrassed man does with that.

My own superficiality complex was compounded when I became a minister and older church leaders advised me, "You can't have friends in the church." A system of moving around the country every few years didn't make for easy depth of friendships either. You were mostly just arriving or getting ready to go (how this was supposed to model Christian community is anyone's guess). You learned to keep a professional distance. I went to a leadership conference and heard the expert say, "You can't lead the people, if you need the people." Sounds catchy, doesn't it? That became my internal mantra. No man is an island? I was Robinson Crusoe—and I didn't even need Man Friday!

I see now how that attitude was so unlike biblical friendship. So unlike Jesus! It is also more dangerous to your health than smoking, and one recent study showed that socially isolated people are twice as likely to have a heart attack. I am so grateful Jesus Christ modeled friendship so differently from the church. When the Son of God left heaven, He came looking for people He could call friends. And of course He did lead them, but He also said at times that He needed them, and He was never afraid to be vulnerable and open with them.

Now it's true none of us can be friends with everyone. Most people are limited to one thousand five hundred faces they can put a name to. My memory is better than that, but I have just moved to a Facebook "Like" page because my time line was filling up with hundreds of acquaintances I didn't really know, and when it comes to friendship, quality trumps quantity all day.

Oxford anthropologist and psychologist Dr. Robin Dunbar says the average number of Christmas card contacts is 150 (thank God for my wife, otherwise nobody would get a card), and that actually your brain can't cope with more than 150 friendships. There's a further limit to how many really close friends you can have. Sociologists suggest that you might invite fifty people to a group dinner, confide in perhaps fifteen people, but rely on five "core" support people, best friends, and family members.[2] Interestingly, these numbers mirror closely how through history armies have formed squadrons, battalions, and teams.

The quality of these relationships will determine your mental and physical well-being. In the age of Twitter and Instagram, the big question is, "Are you spending enough time with your core people, or neglecting them as you try to build the crowd?" What relationships are really most important in your life, and is that reflected in whom you invest yourself in most, in terms of time and energy?

The Bible says that when God became a man, He formed a band of brothers. There were three with whom He was very close, then twelve He lived with 24/7, sharing everything, then seventy with whom He spent a lot of time. Three of them were closer than brothers, certainly closer than His own flesh and blood. He didn't just come to have connection at a distance: He called His disciples friends (John 15:15). He was intimate and vulnerable—He washed their feet—and was betrayed by one of them with a kiss!

How do we get to a deeper level of friendship? A friend of mine, Andy, is a missionary, doing incredible work in Nigeria. Someone who believes in his work bought him a car to help his ministry. One day Andy pulled up to preach at a church here in the UK, and a little boy sitting on the wall of the car park said, "That's a nice car."

"Oh, my friend gave me this car," Andy replied.

The little boy said, "I wish I could *be* a friend like that."

Notice he didn't say, "I wish I had a friend like that."

How often do we think, "How do I get good friends?" rather than, "How do I get to be a friend like that?"

I'm further challenged about friendships when I look at the life of one of the central characters of the New Testament, removed from us in time and geography but still a man we can learn much from because of his tremendously rich relational life. His network was forged despite an incredible schedule of travel, while he went through persecution, problems, and prison. He was incredibly effective in his life mission, but not at the expense of building close, mutually loving, supportive relationships and friendships.

The apostle Paul was effective in his mission but, he also was successful in terms of his relational life. How many men can say that? Paul came a long way, because before he was converted he hated Christians! A violent and angry man may have allies, but not true friends. Yet, when he came to know Jesus Christ on that now famous Damascus road, something changed in his heart because of that primary relationship. Consequently, all his relationships changed too.

The New Testament preserves for us many of the letters Paul wrote to churches. They contain great teaching, encouragement, and occasional rebuke. Often he lists names of friends. It's not like the "cc" or "bcc" list on an email, it is heartfelt. For example, check out Romans 16. I won't include everyone here because I want to comment on a few in particular, but Paul wanted to make sure nobody was left out, and he had an inspiring and appreciative word for all his friends:

> *Say hello to Priscilla and Aquila, who have worked hand in hand with me in serving Jesus. They once put their lives on the line for me. And I'm not the only one grateful to them. All the non-Jewish gatherings of believers also owe them plenty, to say nothing of the church that meets in their house.*
>
> *Hello to my dear friend Epenetus. He was the very first follower of Jesus in the province of Asia.*
>
> *Hello to Mary. What a worker she has turned out to be!*
>
> *Hello to my cousins Andronicus and Junias. We once shared a jail cell. They were believers in Christ before I was. Both of them are outstanding leaders.*
>
> *Hello to Ampliatus, my good friend in the family of God.*
>
> *Hello to Urbanus, our companion in Christ's work, and my good friend Stachys.*
>
> *Hello to Apelles, a tried-and-true veteran in following Christ.*
>
> Romans 16:3–10 (MSG)

I get the impression that wherever he went, even though we know he had a lot of enemies, Paul was great at making and keeping friends—different kinds of friendships with all kinds of people.

I have something to learn from a man like that. These people are not "Facebook friends," where the more you have the less you connect. He knows and is known, he loves and is loved, he cares and is cared for, he prays and is prayed for.

This chapter won't finish with a list of questions, but instead I will describe various types of friendships and ask you to think deeply about your own relationships. Do you have a friend like that? More importantly, could you be a friend like that?

A FRIENDSHIP TO DIE FOR

Near the top of singleton Paul's list are a married couple, Priscilla and Aquila. Paul says they risked their lives for him. I don't know any heroic detail, but that's a deep level of loving friendship.

There are only a few men I could say that about in my own experience, from my days in the cops. One of them, "Big Johnny," remains my best friend. We became Christ followers independently around the same time (he really needed it!), but five years together walking the toughest beat in Manchester at the worst of times made us the best of friends for life.

It was my privilege to conduct the wedding of his daughter, and that night at the reeption I spoke with ex-colleagues and remembered others. Johnny came to my wedding with a black eye after being the first officer injured at the start of what became documented as the Cheetham Hill riots. We went through thick and thin (he was thick, I was thin).

I was never shot at, except with a crossbow bolt, but I've had every other foul thing thrown at me—including a fridge from a high-rise block of apartments! We locked step and kept going. Everyone agreed that the friendships forged in the good old bad old days made for indissoluble bonds. Putting your life on the line for someone is an extraordinary measure of friendship. This will resonate with anyone who has been in the forces for a good length of time.

The first time I heard the Bible's message explained in a way I could relate to was when a great preacher called Eric Delve held a nail in the air, saying, "This is a Roman nail, discovered near Hadrian's

Wall. It's around two thousand years old. This is the kind of nail that would have been driven into Jesus' hands and feet. If someone had to have a nail driven into them, who do you love enough that you would say, 'Don't do it to them, do it to me instead'?"

At the time I was far from God. Some of the things I had witnessed in the job made me strongly doubt He even existed. I was only there because a girl had invited me, but it was an interesting question and my mind whirred. I went through a list to see who would make the cut:

The girl who'd brought me to hear the speaker? Gorgeous, but no. I hardly knew her at the time (now we're married and I'd give a different answer).

My dad? No—he's tougher than me; he could handle it better.

My brother? (We weren't getting on that well at the time.) No. Better him than me!

My sister? Maybe. Probably.

Finally, I picked one person I was sure of. My mum. I'd do it for my mum.

The place was packed but Eric seemed to look me right in the eye as he said, "If you picked anyone, it would have to be someone who you really loved. Jesus did it for you. He said He was doing this for you. Because of your sins, He was taking the punishment you deserve so you could be forgiven. That nail shows how much God loves you."

I was nailed by that statement.

I'd heard the basics of the gospel message since I was a child, but I had rejected what I thought it was. "Jesus died for the sins of the world." So what? Irrelevant. They're still happening, people are still sinning, so it didn't work.

I was one of the good guys, so I didn't need this. I knew from the police, better than most, that there are a lot of bad people in the world. Hearing such a message probably comforted some, I thought. I hoped it didn't comfort the worst (who deserved all they got). I wasn't sad, bad, or needy. I never thought I needed God's love. Until that moment when it was explained in those terms.

I didn't accept the message there and then, but now I knew it was personal. This wasn't about the sins of the world but the sins of Anthony no-middle-name Delaney. The offer of new life and forgiveness—going from being an enemy of God to being a friend— the offer had my name on it. The heroic deed had been done, the ultimate love demonstrated. I could accept or reject this love, but ignoring it was no longer an option, because now I'd finally begun to understand it.

I somehow managed to shrug the power of that challenge off that night and walk out as if life could just carry on the same. But I can recall that message nearly three decades later with perfect clarity, and the reason the message hit so hard was that I really did know what it is to have friends willing to lay down their life for you. Not everyone; some would rather stay safe, thanks very much. But some of the blokes I worked closely with—Jimmy, Fitzy, Lloydy, and others—were men I had formed a bond with by going through doors together and not knowing what or who was on the other side. Some hairy, scary times, fighting alongside someone at a football match or in a pub brawl with everyone throwing pint pots at you, let you know who your mates are.

Priscilla and Aquila had at some point gone to that level for Paul. Putting their lives on the line. I don't know if anyone—other than Jesus Christ—has ever done it for you?

Who would you be willing to take a nail or even a bullet for? Perhaps that will help you think now about your own inner circle, but it takes a lot to build that kind of friendship. We can see how it developed for Paul by reading how he first connected with Priscilla and Aquila in the book of Acts, chapter 18, when he was a stranger in the city of Corinth.

I'll highlight a few passages as we go through and see if you agree with me that as we look at the various friendships Paul developed and enjoyed, the key is *sharing*:

> *Paul left Athens and went to Corinth. There he met a Jew named Aquila, a native of Pontus, who had recently come from Italy with his wife Priscilla, because Claudius had ordered all Jews to leave Rome. Paul went to see them, and because he was a tentmaker as they were, he stayed and worked with them.*
> Acts 18:1–3

SHARED EXPERIENCE

If you want to find a friend, look for common ground. Things we share in common can build and strengthen our relationships. Paul, Aquila, and Priscilla had a shared experience, not an easy one. They had recently come to the large, wealthy city of Corinth from different places in the Roman empire. Strangers in town with different accents. Paul had recently arrived; so had they. A shared experience. Not much of a connection? Enough for Paul to build on.

Paul made the first move. That's important to notice! Sometimes we sit around waiting for everyone to come and befriend us, but I believe, by the grace of God, even the most introverted person can learn to be the first to walk across the room and extend a hand of friendship, kick off a conversation, remember a name, pay attention, ask questions to draw out the other person (as Disraeli must have done rather than talk about himself), and find common ground—rather than expecting someone to do it to us. Be a friend like that!

Their shared experience included that they were all going through a similar tough time. Paul later wrote that when he arrived in Corinth, it was "with great fear and trembling" (1 Cor. 2:3). Wherever Paul went, trouble followed. His passion divided opinion. He kicked fences and as a result was often going from one kind of trouble to a different sort of bother, particularly with the authorities. Priscilla and Aquila had just been thrown out of Rome because the emperor was disturbed by the fear of riots, as so many Jews were turning to follow one they called "Christus."

They shared a Jewish heritage. We don't know whether Priscilla and Aquila were Christ followers before they met Paul, but they did have some things in common. Not everything, but enough. When you are looking for friendships it is good to look at what you have in common—don't just focus on the differences. Paul was single, they were married. Maybe they were different ages. They originated from different countries. Paul could have thought, "They are too different, why bother?" Instead he saw that it is good to mix it up a little! Single people—don't just have single friends! Married people—don't just have married friends! Mix it up. They had shared experiences and common ground.

SHARED WORK

The three had something else in common. Paul was a tentmaker, as they were. He stayed and worked with them, and they became business partners.

Studies from the Department of Obvious Facts show that working environments where people feel they are engaged in tasks together with friends, rather than just colleagues, are less stressful and far more productive. (Okay, I made this one up, but I wouldn't be surprised if someone did pay inordinate amounts of money to prove it.)

Do you have friends or just colleagues in the workplace? You can have great friendships at work if you show yourself to be a person of integrity, honesty, and someone who isn't going to bad-mouth or gossip like everybody else. If you can be reliable, others will start to rely on you. People want a friend like that. Like the man Walt Mason described:

> There's a man in the world who is never turned down, wherever he chances to stray; he gets the glad hand in the populous town, or out where the farmers make hay; he's greeted with pleasure on deserts of sand, and deep in the aisles of the woods: wherever he goes there's the welcoming hand—he's The Man Who Delivers the Goods.[3]

SHARED HOME

Paul, Priscilla, and Aquila even shared a home together, which can either make or break a friendship! Over the years our family has been incredibly enriched by opening up our home to have various people and even whole families come to live with us, some just for a short term and some for several months. It's rare for us not to have someone living with us who has become part of the family.

The Bible encourages us that when you open up your home, you could find you are entertaining angels unawares (Heb. 13:2). Though I don't think we've ever had any angels, we have got some great friends as a result of that—people who have stayed the course over many years.

SHARED PASSION

Silas and Timothy were friends like that to Paul: "When Silas and Timothy came from Macedonia, Paul devoted himself exclusively to preaching, testifying to the Jews that Jesus was the Messiah" (Acts 18:5).

Paul worked as a tentmaker—but that was how he made a living, not what he lived for. Silas and Timothy had been delayed in another city, but as soon as his old mates turned up and joined him in town, he was fired up by their shared passion to help people find their way back to God, and they went at it full-time. They had quite a history together. Silas had been in a Macedonian prison with Paul, not because they were criminals but because they had been arrested for preaching about Christ since it was considered illegal, as it still is in many places around the world today. They had even been through an earthquake together.

I don't know how you can arrange it to happen—and actually the more I think about it I really wouldn't recommend the strategy—but when you have been through an earthquake with somebody you end up becoming better friends.

On many occasions over the years I have visited Haiti, the poorest country in the Western Hemisphere, because of the great relief, aid, and child support work of Compassion International, for which I am a passionate advocate. The third time I went was with my pal Andy Hawthorne—founder and director of *The Message Trust*—to bring emergency medical aid and food packages to field hospitals within days of the terrible earthquake of 2010 that killed hundreds of thousands and displaced over one million.[4]

We helped people who had been pulled out of the rubble and drove them to field hospitals and did whatever we could and whatever was needed. Andy and I went through earthquake tremors—aftershocks—every day we were out there. On one occasion it happened when Andy was sitting on the toilet! The whole building he was in at a makeshift hospital started to shake. We'd been told that if whatever building you are in starts to shake, you have a maximum of fifteen seconds to get out. He was still counting and debating whether to pull his trousers up when, thankfully, the tremor stopped.

I know he'll be grateful that I shared that story with you. It's what friends are for.

Paul and Silas had a past together and a shared passion for the gospel. Andy and I had known each other as acquaintances for twenty years or more, but a visit to Haiti with our wives a year before demonstrated to us both that we shared a passion to connect ordinary people, especially the poorest of the poor, to the life-changing God who loves them. We went to a whole new level by going through a time when the world wobbles. When you're utterly dependent on God for shelter, protection, and miraculous provision (and find how He comes through for you), it only increases that desire to make a difference in the world with this one short life.

SHARED MENTORING

Timothy was a younger guy that Paul was mentoring. They had become very close, though in age they were a generation or two apart. Paul had been mentoring Priscilla and Aquila too, but he called Timothy his "son," treated him like one, and invested in his life.

So many younger men are longing for you older guys reading this to be willing to open up your hearts, homes, schedules, and lives, to be men who will share not just your successes but your struggles. They want to know how others who have gone before them learned, overcame, and carried on.

If only more older men were willing to share such life lessons. I could fill a stadium with younger guys longing for that. Our fractured and fatherless society could be transformed by a mentoring movement like that. It's the key to holistic life success. Introduce me to a successful man, and I will ask him who mentored him to get him there.

Too many young men are literally dying for lack of someone to pray for them, believe in them, and speak a timely word of encouragement to them. You can't do that with everybody and neither can I, but in the last seven years I have turned my life focus around to make that more and more a possibility so I can leave a greater legacy in the lives of others.

Are you doing this with anyone? I now mentor many men, and I am also mentored by a number of other wiser men—not necessarily older—who have walked the road further and better than me. Are you actively seeking out some men that you can do that with? Giving and receiving. You are not responsible to fill their cup, but you are responsible to empty yours. You don't have to wait any longer. Who are you pouring your life into that way? What's the qualification? If you can love, you can mentor.

It's good that Paul had friends like this because as you read on you'll see that when he preaches in Corinth it doesn't go too well. He has friends, but he also has some enemies, who became abusive. There are lots of people who like me, I am pleased to say. But I know there are also some people who don't like me (I can live with that; I don't even like me sometimes!). Paul wasn't intentionally going around making enemies, but he had learned how to cope with that. He didn't stop trying to make friends just because he had been rejected. What did he do?

> *Then Paul left the synagogue and went next door to the house of Titius Justus, a worshiper of God. Crispus, the synagogue leader, and his entire household believed in the Lord; and many of the Corinthians who heard Paul believed and were baptized.*
> Acts 18:7–8

SHARED LOCALITY

Somebody might reject you, but right next to them there's often somebody looking for a friend like you! We are just not looking in the right place. The next set of great friends God had lined up for Paul were living right next door. They shared the neighborhood together.

Some people sit around in the house wishing they had loads of friends but don't go and initiate any friendships, even with the people next door. Paul saw the world differently from most of us, who think where we live just happens. When Paul was in Athens, he told people he met there that where you live right now is no accident—it is God's plan! Paul came to understand that God "marked out their appointed times in history and the boundaries of their lands. God did this so that they would seek him and perhaps reach out for him and find him, though he is not far from any one of us" (Acts 17:26, 27).

Everything changes when I begin to see that there are people living on my street, or moving in soon, that God put there so I get to share something of my life with them and can help them find their way back to God—not by putting "Jesus loves you" posters in my windows, but just by being the best possible neighbor I can be.

My father-in-law told me he'd met a guy who lived opposite me years ago. I used to be friendly to him—mainly because he was a professional boxer and a bit of a scary character. I didn't even know his name; I just called him Boss! He said to my father-in-law, "Are you related to Anthony? Anthony Delaney?" He bravely admitted that was the case, hoping I didn't owe the guy money.

"Tell him I'm a Christian now," he said. "I never was when he lived opposite and was my neighbor, but now I am. Tell him I will never forget what he said to me that day when I was washing my car."

Well, I'm glad he'll never forget what I said, because I certainly can't remember! I don't even remember having the conversation, but I do remember we both shared a street, and God somehow used something to draw this man to reach out and find Him there.

SHARED JOURNEY

Paul stayed on in Corinth for some time. Then he left the brothers and sisters and sailed for Syria, accompanied by Priscilla and Aquila. . . . They arrived at Ephesus, where Paul left Priscilla and Aquila. He himself went into the synagogue and reasoned with the Jews. When they asked him to spend more time with them, he declined. But as he left, he promised, "I will come back if it is God's will."
Acts 18:18–21

The trouble got worse and then a little better in Corinth before Paul moved on, but he didn't do so alone. Priscilla and Aquila shared the journey, then he left them.

There are some people with whom you share the journey and become friends with along the way. Then you say goodbye, and that's okay. You will bump into them again and it will be as if you only saw them yesterday.

Remember my earlier sad tale of friendship lost with Paul Marshall—the boy I used to dream of doing comic books with using my words and his art? We reconnected a couple of years back completely out of the blue on Facebook. Turns out he is now an award-winning comic artist who has worked for Marvel and is now one of the chief cover artists for *Judge Dredd* and therefore the coolest friend in the world. We met up after decades apart and then made the dream come true by collaborating to produce resources together where I did the writing and he provided fantastic cover art.

People come and people go and sometimes they come back. There have been times we have moved on to the next stage of the adventure of following God and people have gotten very upset that we went or that we were not going to be part of the journey with them anymore. There are people I have been friends with for a while and then they have gone off on a different part of the journey. Their lives have gone in one direction and mine has gone in another and that is okay—nobody has to fall out, we can still be friends. I don't have to feel rejected and hurt about that. I don't own anyone, and they don't owe me anything.

> The main thing that you have to remember on this journey
> is, just be nice to everyone and always smile.
> —attributed to Ed Sheeran

Paul shared his time with some new people at Ephesus, but then there came a point when he said, "Thanks, but no." Paul was a busy guy with demands from all kinds of people asking him to stay with them—sometimes he said no. The most effective people realize we have to say no even to good people and good things to do God's best for us.

Are you any good at saying no? Don't just say no to prove a point now.

Paul said, "I'm off now—and if it's God's will I will come back." Someone else was planning his schedule. He didn't stay there a day longer than he should just to keep them smiling at the expense of following his destiny and doing what he really should have been doing. Just because some people invited you doesn't mean you should go. I need to learn to say, "Maybe, if it is God's will, we'll do that at some point—but not now." Like everybody else, I have 1,440 minutes today and have already slept through a chunk of them, so now there are things I need to do and things I don't need to do.

Most of us suffer more for what we say yes to than what we miss out on. How can we improve? I read an interview way back with Paul Newman where he was asked the most important lesson he'd ever learned. He said it was to be able to say "no" well. He said he used a phrase when he was invited to do something he really shouldn't be doing: "I'm sorry, but that's impossible for me." I imagine him smiling graciously as he used that phrase and found it accepted, because really there's no arguing with it.

I believe nothing is impossible for God, but the job is already taken. I can't do everything or please everyone, so I've used that little phrase time and again and it's got me out of a world of hassle many times, so I pass it on! Say no. Say no to something every day this week, just to practice, and you will soon have more of the right things to say yes to, like building relationships that will have a positive ripple effect, as Paul did:

> *Meanwhile a Jew named Apollos, a native of Alexandria, came to Ephesus. He was a learned man, with a thorough knowledge of the Scriptures. He had been instructed in the way of the Lord, and he spoke with great fervor and taught about Jesus accurately, though he knew only the baptism of John. He began to speak boldly in the synagogue. When Priscilla and Aquila heard him, they invited him to their home and explained to him the way of God more adequately.*
> Acts 18:24–26

Paul had left Priscilla and Aquila, but he left something with them that affected how they did friendship. When an extraordinarily gifted man with some holes in his thinking and theology turned up in their orbit, Priscilla and Aquila made the first move. They welcomed him and shared their home with him. They connected through a shared passion as they lovingly straightened him out, looking at Scripture together. They shared in mentoring to help Apollos grow to be all he could be and do all he was meant to do for God. It rubbed off on Paul—the return on what Paul had invested in them.

Proverbs 27:17 says, "As iron sharpens iron, so one person

sharpens another." Paul shared friendship, which his friends shared with Apollos, who would never have been the man he became without them. This is the way it should work. Paul wrote to friends in a different church, "Because we loved you so much, we were delighted to share with you not only the gospel of God but our lives as well" (1 Thess. 2:8).

It is possible to share the message of God's love but not to share anything of your life? It happens all the time, unfortunately. But what would the church look like if we were known as the friendliest people on earth?

Paul wanted to share not just a message or knowledge, but his life too. He shared experiences, his work, and his home; he shared a passion for his life mission, matched only by his desire to share what mattered most to him with the next generation. Paul encouraged people; he said no to some so that he could say a better yes to others; he mentored people. Is it any wonder he had friends? I wish I could be a friend like that!

A MAN'S BEST FRIEND

If you were to ask Paul—who could list all sorts of friendships—that playground question, "Who's your best friend?" you know who he would say, don't you?

Jesus.

Of course. No hesitation.

Jesus is the perfect example of the friend "who sticks closer than a brother" (Prov. 18:24). I said already that Paul had a hard time in Corinth, where people rejected him and abused him. He was scared and very lonely, at the end of his tether, perhaps wondering if he was in the right place at all.

It is said a friend walks in when everyone else walks out. On that dark night of the soul, Paul's best friend walked in again:

One night the Lord spoke to Paul in a vision: "Do not be afraid; keep on speaking, do not be silent. For I am with you, and no one is going to attack and harm you, because I have many people in this city."
Acts 18:9–10

An old hymn declares, "What a friend we have in Jesus!" It's so true. We all have friends who come and go throughout our lives, but I have a friend who sticks closer than a brother. My best friend is the most powerful VIP in the universe. My best friend promises, "I will never leave you nor forsake you—I want to be your best friend, and once you say yes to Me and I say yes to you, it doesn't matter who might say no to you. I am with you always, so don't be afraid" (see Matt. 28:20; Heb. 13:5).

Isn't that fantastic? It changes everything once you see who Jesus is and hear Him making that offer and promise to you. Who is your best friend? Jesus says He wants to be yours. The offer is the vulnerable moment. You can accept or reject. He offers the kind of friendship that takes a bullet for you. He became ultimately vulnerable on the cross for you. He stretched out His arms wide so He could embrace you in a God-man hug. Will you make Him your best friend? Will you go and befriend others with that same kind of vulnerable love?

That is such an amazing promise! "Do not be afraid, because I am with you." Jesus makes that promise to you and to me. Will you be His best friend? He will be yours.

I spoke with kids in a high school lesson, trying to explain Christianity as best as I could in the half hour they'd given me. A girl sitting at the back chewing gum like you are not supposed to put a hand up, looking very unimpressed.

"So you're telling me, right, that the Bible says, right, that God really, really loves us—and wants to be our friend?" She was smirking by the end, as if this ere the most ridiculous message ever!

I said yes. Because the Twitter generation just summed it up perfectly in under 140 characters.

Karl Barth, one of the greatest theologians ever, with a brain the size of a planet, who wrote massive books of theology, arrived in the United States and was asked by a reporter, "Doctor Barth, after all you have written and studied, what is the most important insight?"

He thought for a moment before answering, "Jesus loves me, this I know, for the Bible tells me so."

A man's best friend is his God.

Chapter 7

Father

"By profession I am a soldier and take pride in that fact. But I am prouder—infinitely prouder—to be a father. . . . It is my hope that my son, when I am gone, will remember me not from the battle but in the home repeating with him our simple daily prayer, 'Our Father Who Art in Heaven.'"

– GENERAL DOUGLAS MACARTHUR

"THE NEAREST THING I can think of to how it feels? Well, it's like when I'm riding my motorbike into a hairpin bend." Noel was speaking slowly, nursing his too-hot coffee in the polystyrene cup. I knew enough not to interrupt. Looking into the cup again, he went on. "You know what you have to do: lean in and keep the power on. But it's scary whenever you approach. So you're tempted to pull out of the turn. That's how it feels."

He was talking about making a decision to become a follower of Jesus Christ, as he'd just seen others do by simply kneeling to pray at the foot of a large cross we'd set up there in the café.

For the last five mornings Noel had come along to the "Just

Looking" sessions at the large Christian conference I was teaching at. While others gathered in large numbers to sing and hear about God, those who had no idea why that first group did so were welcome to talk, question, and respond at the level they felt ready for. We had looked at various movie clips, listened to people's real-life stories, and with lots of questions looked at what the Bible had to say about how ordinary people can connect to God.

Noel wasn't into God. He was into his motorbike. His wife was the "religious" one. Years before, they'd agreed to a deal, a great compromise. She was not ever going to get excited about his Triumph Bonneville T100 and he wasn't interested in singing with a crowd of "God botherers." But if she went to his conventions he would go to her conferences.

Here, and at innumerable other Christian events, he sat outside the tent smoking or taking his bike to bits while she was at seminars. We had set up in the coffee area—he came in, and for some reason was hooked on the sessions from day one. Genuine, intelligent questions followed at the end of every session. His wife couldn't believe he was there every single day. She never wanted to be pushy with her faith; she loved him as he was no matter what, but she was praying very hard for the man she loved!

"So what makes you pull out of the bend? What scares you about becoming a Christian?"

"Well, I get Jesus, but I struggle with that whole 'Our Father' bit for a start," said Noel.

I should have guessed. With many of the men I've talked to that are the hardest to reach, particularly those who would identify strongly as atheists, I cut through the intellectual smoke screen and various pseudo-questions by simply asking, "What kind of relationship do you have with your dad?"

The range of responses is not very wide:

"Who? Never knew him."

"Critical, picky, unpleaseable—that would be on a good day."

"We just stay out of each other's way—it's for the best."

Your first reference point, map, and compass for manhood is, or was, your father. Dead or alive, present or absent, good or bad, he colors your view of yourself, your attitude to older men, and—crucially—to God. Suppress or deny it as you may, this matters. If you could not connect with or trust him, that will carry over relationally, emotionally, developmentally, and, yes, spiritually. This is a bedrock of child psychology, the need for love and approval. If you never had your father directly praise you or lovingly hold you to demonstrate his approval, you will long for and look for substitutes for that throughout your life. Or you will shut that part of yourself down and carry the wound.

Noel continued, looking over at the cross. "The words 'relationship' and 'dad' are an oxymoron. He was there, but not—you know what I mean? So I hear about Jesus, and I'm interested. When you talk about the cross, I'm drawn somehow. But when you say it's happening so I could come to God the Father . . . no. Not interested. Why would I want a God who is a Father?"

In *The Knowledge of the Holy*, A. W. Tozer wrote, "What comes to our minds when we think about God is the most important thing about us. . . . Were we able to extract from any man a complete answer to the question, 'What comes to mind when you think about God?' we might predict with certainty the spiritual future of that man."[1]

I put a note out on my Facebook page asking for people to play word association and tell me their first reaction to the word *father*. Within minutes I had a remarkable series of responses. Most but not all of those who responded were Christians. Let me read them to you:

FATHER =

- Strength
- Affirmer
- Sat on his knee, warm, safe, and protected (when I was a kid this was, mind you)
- Secure
- Warmth
- First reaction is to smile! Then this picture of the open arms of the Father, my heavenly Father, just waiting to gather me up in an embrace.
- Fun
- Gentle, gentleman
- Steadfast, reliable, protector
- Solid

Sounds great? No problem then.

But that was only the responses of the women.

I know this is a random and not a scientific sample, and I don't want to over-egg it. One or two men had some positive reactions, as I would have. A few men made jokes like "Father . . . Christmas" or "Ted." But while *none* of the women's reactions were negative, the contrast with the men's was pretty stark (some people emailed me rather than publicly posting):

FATHER =

- Liar
- Cheat
- Absent
- Evil
- Just wanted him to say he's proud of me

- Fear
- Hangman
- Distance
- Authoritarian bad guy who scares the living **** out of you!
- Ignoring

Gordon Dalbey, author of *Healing the Masculine Soul*, recounts that nun in a men's prison once helped a prisoner purchase a Mother's Day card for him to send out, but when she did, she found herself deluged by requests from inmates. She contacted Hallmark Cards, who kindly obliged by donating cards.

As Father's Day drew near, she was better prepared. The warden duly announced that free cards could be collected from the chapel, yet not even one prisoner asked for a Father's Day card.[2]

What the men's movement calls "the father wound" and others call "the fatherless crisis" is perhaps the biggest single challenge the church in the West has to face if it is to stem the hemorrhaging of men from its ranks. How might that miracle happen? By churches re-creating a sense of family, men rising up to be surrogate fathers, and by reclaiming the biblical doctrine of adoption—that God's own Son came and gave up His place in the family so that we could know God as Father.

Jesus Christ knew the love of a perfect heavenly Father and an imperfect earthly one. One day He eyed a crowd He identified as imperfect fathers. Even the best would be included in that number. He asked hypothetically, "Which of you, if your son asks for bread, will give him a stone? Or if he asks for a fish, will give him a snake?" (Matt. 7:9–10).

While I think this (together with many other of His sayings) points up Jesus' great comic timing, the picture it paints is appalling. A son comes looking for what he needs but is offered or receives something useless, cruel, or even harmful.

Many of our fathers were doing their level best, but how many boys came to dad looking for a hug but were told he was "too busy right now" and received aloneness instead of affection? Worse still (as I think of some of the most broken men I have befriended and mentored), some even received and survived horrific abuse, even sexual abuse. They got boulders for bread, serpents instead of salmon.

THE WAY HOME

You probably know the story; Dickens called it the greatest short story ever told. A young man lives in a great home with a wonderful father, but as he grows up he can't see it. He breaks Dad's heart with five words: "I wish you were dead." His style is cramped; he was made for the city. Let the lame duck older brother stay and look after the farm; he can't go one more day looking at fat calves and fixing farm machines. "Give me my share of the inheritance I'd get after your funeral; I can't wait for you to die."

A parent knows that you can't keep them when they decide to go, no matter how much you want or try to. Rather than shout, spank, or scold, the father does it. He liquidates half of his assets, converts it into cold cash, and weeps as his son turns his back and walks away without a word.

The boy's a high roller for a while. Wine, women, and song—and he doesn't do much singing. But when the ventures fail, the adventure's stale and the friends bail. He ends up doing the only job he's qualified for, farm laborer. This good Jewish boy is now in charge of pigswill, with a boss who treats the porkers better than the workers.

But one day, when what the pigs are eating starts to look appealing, he has one of those "there must be more to life than this" moments. "What am I doing here? How did it get to this? If I went home, Dad could at least put me in charge of his animals!"

He composes a fine speech, rehearses the perfect tone of contrition, thinks of a few religious phrases to spice it up. Then tells his boss exactly where to stick the shovel and gets walking.

It's a long journey home. Days in the blazing sun, baking on the stink from the pigs. He is tired out, thirsty, and starving, but nobody will give him anything. Raging with thirst, nearer death than he knows, he finally sees the old place. There's noise inside from some kind of celebration, whiffs of something cooking that drive him crazy, even at this distance. He knocks on the door. His father opens it.

"Dad, I . . . I'm so sorry . . . I have been a fool. I've wasted it all . . . I should have listened . . ."

The old man replies, "Do I know you? No. I do not know you. I only have one son—he is a good boy; he lives here with me. It is his birthday party today. I once had another son, a younger one, but he died many years ago. Get off my porch or I'll get my gun. Go back to wherever you came from."

The door slams in his face.

Now, if you know anything at all about the Bible, you will be getting frustrated now because you know that's not how the story ends. At least you think you know that's not how it ends. But once upon a time, for a very long time, the story would have ended like that.

Some scholars believe that the rabbis and Pharisees, the religious teachers of the Law in Jesus' day, used to tell that story to warn people, especially, but not exclusively, the kids.[3] "Don't you ever step out of line. Don't presume on God's patience. He is a holy, stern God and He has chosen you to be in His house. His rules and laws must not be trifled with. If you want to have a relationship with Him, stand up straight and live right. Or else there's no way back. He's that kind of God."

But Jesus knew His Dad so much better. So Jesus came and

changed the ending. No wonder they wanted to kill Him. He changed one of their best stories! The kind of teaching religion loves was totally spoiled—by grace.

Jesus redirects the characters and creates a final scene with a picture of a different kind of father. He has been looking out for his lost son and longing for him to come home so much and for so long that when he glimpses him at a distance, he leaves aside all pretense at dignity on the doorstep and runs up the driveway. He picks up the skirts of his robes and runs (fathers then would never run—terribly unseemly). He hugs his son so tightly, ferociously kisses the apology half-mumbled off his mouth. He gives him back everything he had squandered so recklessly—robe, ring, sandals—the signs and insignia of a son. Here is a father who does not lecture but lavishes, who does not castigate but celebrates his son's return with a party.

What kind of an ending is that?!

Religion knows nothing of that kind of an ending. I love that kind an ending. Since I became a Christ follower I've been a sucker for it. No, before I came to know God as Father like that, I think it may have been hardwired into me—and into you too. This is meant to be our story, which explains why some of the stories and movies that most pull at our hearts are excerpts or remakes of that old script.

Let me share something with you. It's not the kind of thing blokes normally share, but by now maybe we're closer than we were. It's about what makes me cry.

When I was about seven, I sat with my mum and watched a film on TV called *Shenandoah*. It's what I used to think of as a Saturday afternoon movie, one of those interminably long epics that lasted right up until sponge pudding and custard before the wrestling and football results came on ("Forfar four, East Fife five").

James Stewart plays Charlie Anderson, a landowner with six sons. The American Civil War looms closer to his homestead in the

South, and despite his determination to protect them, his family—his boys—are inexorably drawn into the conflict, one by one.

Various intertwined plots play out, one of which involves the youngest son, referred to only as "Boy," being mistakenly taken prisoner. Anderson sets off to look for him and bring him back, but the son is lost, pressed into fighting in the conflict before being shot in a battle.

All afternoon goes by and the sponge pudding knocks in the pan as the film draws to a close at the wedding of another of his sons. The shadow of Boy's absence hangs over the celebrations. Until . . . the church doors burst open! What's this? Unbelievable! On crutches, not dead—alive! The lost son! He's here! The father sets off running.

I set off crying. Bawling. In bits.

I'll never forget the first time I saw that film and how much I cried, and my mum never let me forget either.

When I was sixteen it was on again, and I thought I could handle it now that I was a Police Cadet. I did, until the church doors burst open—and then I started bawling like a baby.

I'm in my mid-twenties, married now. Working as a cop on a tough inner-city beat, soon going to be on the Riot Squad. Flicking through the channels at home. There it is. "Guess what, Zoe, this film that's on, *Shenandoah*, I watched it when I was a kid. Ha! It made me cry when I was a kid. Let's watch it."

Bad move. Very bad move.

I know to stay well away from that film if I want to retain my street cred. My mother sent me a text just the other day with a smiley face on it to tell me "*Shenandoah* is on this weekend." Thanks, Mum.

Finding Nemo got me too, nearly as badly. The lost son, the father who goes all out on a search and rescue. Reunion. Celebration. Even though it's animated clownfish, I'm hardwired to respond in a lachrymal way to that kind of story.

I'm on a plane with my daughter. I opt for *The Lion, the Witch and the Wardrobe.* Bad move. The bit that really gets me? Greedy Edmund who has betrayed his friends. Stupid, annoying Edmund who caused all the trouble is led into the palace and crowned. Aslan himself declares him to be not what he was, but what he has become: "Prince Edmund—the Just!"

Whoa! Here I go! "Dad, you're so embarrassing!"

All those prodigal stories hook my heart and squeeze tears out because I know from my own life experience what it is to be really very lost—and then very loved by the real God, not the one I had rejected.

DAD

Let me try another word association with you: GOD.

Your first response will tell a lot about what you think of Him. But I'll try another tack: what did God think about you when you opened your eyes this morning?

Do you think He was ashamed of you? He knows what you have thought, done, and said. Was He angry? Is God waiting to judge you? Is He like a drill sergeant, waiting to line you up to inspect you? If so, that is a problem. The Bible doesn't just invite but *commands* that you love the Lord your God with all your heart, mind, soul, and strength (Matt. 22:37). How do you command an emotion? Especially when it would have to be hard to love a god like that. You can respect or reject, fear or flee from a god like that all right, but love him? Tall order.

When you stepped into the bathroom and looked at that man in the mirror, what did God see? A disappointment? Would He prefer you to just go back to bed rather than go and mess up again?

Perhaps God didn't even notice you woke up. He's got a lot going on. Over 125 billion galaxies, all those planets to spin and stars to count. What's your little life? Why should it matter? Why would you matter to Him? If God is aloof, apathetic, indifferent, it's hard to love a god like that, even if he commands it.

No wonder so many people reject a god like that.

I rejected that god when I was a teenager and I reject him today too, because that's not the real God. That's not the God I know. The God and Father of our Lord Jesus Christ.

When you woke this morning, God was wide awake. The real God was watching you like the most besotted father who ever drooled over a newborn on its first night in a cot. Every time you rolled over, scratched, or snored, He saw you in the dark, with love in His eyes. The real God loves you unconditionally. He's crazy about you. He doesn't like all the things you do because they hurt you and others, and there are consequences to many of them that break His heart, but He still thinks you're fantastic. Nothing will change that, because He cannot change.

The real God could not wait till you woke up, so you could connect with Him and then join in with Him in His work in the world. The real God is like the best dad but a billion times better, with love a trillion times stronger and more faithful. That's the real God: super excited to love you!

Here's how one early Jesus follower described how he felt about his relationship (not his religion—there's a massive difference!) with God:

> *See what great love the Father has lavished on us, that we should be called children of God! And that is what we are!*
> 1 John 3:1

Changing how you see God changes how you see yourself and everything. Did you notice that word *lavished*? I love that word! What a picture! You have a heavenly Father who goes OTT, all out, full on. He lays it on thick. He'd rather spoil you with love than spoil you by not loving you.

Did you ever think God could be a dad like that? The real God is. He's put His heart right out there. He wrote His love in a book for you to find it in case you missed it in every sunrise and sunset. His love leaves nothing unsaid. What a contrast with so many imperfect earthly father-son relationships.

No earthly father is perfect, but I was immensely privileged to be the son of Enri Gilmore Delaney. He went back to God a decade ago now, but I miss him every day. The onset of cancer too soon (it always is) meant there were a few months for late-night long talks and nothing left unsaid between us. The morphine kept him silent for days, and I took shifts with my brother and sister to sit with him on his bed as he was dying, playing his favorite music collections with no discernible response. I sang along to Bob Marley's "Three Little Birds," but the emotion was cracking my voice and it sounded terrible.

"Sorry, Dad, not much of a singer."

"I love to hear you sing." His last words to me. Total approval, unconditional love.

"Paddy" was the funniest, toughest, kindest man. He worked in various manual jobs though he had one of the finest minds of anyone I have ever met, rattling off crosswords in no time and answering all the questions on TV quiz shows without a pause. He was a father who lavished the love on thick in my life, which helps me understand the real God in a way I know many men cannot fully understand.

One of my earliest memories was when I was six years of age. Dad worked with vats of industrial chemicals in a factory in those pre–health and safety days and was badly burned all over his body by caustic soda. Hospitalized for weeks, he couldn't have visitors. I missed him terribly, until I came home from school one day to find him lying on the couch under a thin sheet, sent home to recover. I was told not to touch him; it would hurt him.

So I stood there twitching, shuffling from foot to foot.

He stretched out toward me. No way I was going to stand there without a hug!

"Come on, Son, come for your hug."

I knew it hurt him. He did too, though he would never show it. I will never, never, never forget lying fully stretched out on his body. My head went on his chest; I listened to his heartbeat and his words of affirmation as he stroked my hair. I knew what it was to be completely loved. Love was defined for me that afternoon. I was his little boy. I had done nothing to deserve that kind of love, but I was so glad to just soak it all up.

I have told that story in various settings and seen crowds of men cry. So many would do anything (some do kill) for want of love like that from a father. I know how incredibly rare and precious it is, receiving that kind of love from an earthly dad. I want to love my kids like that. If you never got that love, that does not have to stop you from loving your kids like that.

Whether your earthly dad was awesome, absent, or awful, I have good news for you. You can be adopted. A perfect heavenly Father has chosen to do everything it took to choose you and bring you into His family forever. It has been terribly painful for Him, but God wanted you to be loved like that, as close as a heartbeat, now and forever. You have to come to Him because you will only know who you are when you know *whose* you are. He reaches out to you now, where you are. He is there; He will never not care. He is not too busy. He wants you to hear the same words He told your older brother Jesus before He sent Him to come and bring you home—before He ever performed a miracle or preached a sermon: "You are my Son, whom I love; with you I am well pleased" (Mark 1:11).

Imagine what it feels like to be in such a royal family! Can you imagine how your life could change if you allowed your identity to be transformed by being adopted like that? By the God-Father who throws a party when you return to Him? By the One that Jesus said you can call by the same name He uses when He talks to Him: "Abba"—Daddy!

> *How blessed is God! And what a blessing he is! He's the Father of our Master, Jesus Christ, and takes us to the high places of blessing in him. Long before he laid down earth's foundations, he had us in mind, had settled on us as the focus of his love, to be made whole and holy by his love. Long, long ago he decided to adopt us into his family through Jesus Christ.*
> Ephesians 1:3–5 (MSG)

Many dear friends and people close to us have adopted a child. It's a miracle. Everything changes. New name, new identity, it's legally binding forever. They are Mum and Dad. That's their job. They chose to love. The child's job? Be loved. Be adopted. Receive it. Believe it. Enjoy it.

Who are you? You are who He says you are. Try saying it, out loud, where you are.

"I am the son of my heavenly Father. He loves me. He is well pleased with me."

Healthy societies have recognized the vital role of fathers since the most ancient times, and despite the best efforts of trendy social engineers, anyone with their head in the real world knows that dads are irreplaceable in forming a son from boy to man.

The best mother would admit that there are some things even she cannot do. Men need to be around older men to learn the answer to the question of what it really is to be a man or they'll go to all the wrong places and people, make it up, and get it wrong. That's why mentoring and cross-generational relationships have to be intentionally put in place, so we can see some real men—men who are authentic, live with integrity, and finish well. Even the best dads are imperfect; they can't teach all you need to know.

For example, some dads love to teach their sons about how to fix things practically. My father-in-law was from an engineering background and taught his son how all the tools worked to fix the car or washing machine. It helped that his son was practical, whereas I'm a klutz.

My dad had a toolbox in the shed, but it was this mysterious, wonderful but incomprehensible treasure trove he would only open occasionally. He didn't teach me too much about the contents or how to work them, which may well be the reason I put the Idiot in DIY. He taught me more important lessons like hard work, good social skills, and how to read before I went to school—so I figured out how to read the Yellow Pages or call in a favor to get someone else to fix the car or washing machine.

THE FATHER'S TOOLBOX

Now that I've been adopted by my heavenly Dad, there are lessons He wants to teach me in how to be a man every day. He made a purpose-filled, joyful life for me and opens His toolbox to show me how it works and how to fix it when things go wrong. Have a peek with me inside.

HAMMER AND CHISEL

Search online for "The Skit Guys" and watch their short drama sketch "God's Chisel." Right after a man prays a simple prayer inviting God to change him, God appears right alongside him with a hammer and chisel. After hilariously establishing the true identity of the visitor, our man submits to the change program, until it hurts. Then control kicks in.

He resists.

Complains.

Justifies.

Points to others worse than him. Any of that familiar?

I am precious to God, but I still have a lot of rough edges that need to be knocked off before God has me ready for His perfection in heaven. I'm like Michelangelo's *David*, trapped inside a lump of marble needing to be set free by the master sculptor, while my Father sees the image of His true Son and wants me to bear the family likeness. He goes to work with the chisel, and if pain comes I may take it as evidence that He's losing interest, the power to change me, or love for me—the opposite is true! You may have been subjected to unfair treatment by your earthly father, but your adopting Dad would never do that:

> *The* LORD *disciplines those he loves, as a father the son he delights in.*
> Proverbs 3:12

But ouch—the chisel hurts! I don't want that bit chipped away at, not today anyway!

> *No discipline seems pleasant at the time, but painful. Later on, however, it produces a harvest of righteousness and peace for those who have been trained by it.*
> Hebrews 12:11

SANDPAPER

Sometimes the changes the Father makes in me happen more gently, as He rubs away over time. He knows what He's doing. Remember, He accepts you just as you are but loves you enough not to leave you like that, so He makes you what only He can help you become. There can be sandpaper situations, sandpaper times, and, yes, sandpaper people in your life!

The Bible often talks about desert times. Like many men of God, we're formed in the wilderness wanderings and wastelands. When we're disoriented, thirsty, and hungry, we see what we've been too easily satisfied by. We get more desperate for direction and the bread of angels. That's a good place to be.

Why sandpaper? It's a map of the desert! We can't see the way out, but our Father can and He knows that we'll come out from it changed.

A Native American tribe observes a rite of passage where the boy is taken by his father into the bush, sat on a tree stump, and blindfolded—he must now be left alone. He is required to sit there all night. He must obey the father and not remove the blindfold until the rays of the morning sun shine through it. He cannot cry out for help to anyone. Once (If? Surely the question is there or it's not a real trial) he survives the night, he is a man. The secrets of this ritual are guarded closely—he cannot tell other boys of this experience, because each lad must come into manhood on his own.

The boy is naturally terrified. He can hear all kinds of noises. Wild beasts must surely be surrounding him now. He could be attacked or harmed by man or beast. Wind and leaves play tricks all night, but he must sit wide awake and never remove the blindfold. He must not! This is the only way the boy can become a man!

Finally, after the longest night of his life, the sun appears and the young man removes his blindfold—to discover his father sitting there silently on the stump next to him. He had been at his watch post the entire night, diligently protecting his son. We too are never alone. God has promised to never leave nor forsake us.

We may not know it or feel like it, but Abba Father is watching over us. He never slumbers or sleeps. In the hot or cold desert places we learn that just because you can't see or hear God right now doesn't mean He is not there. Following the sandpaper map means we walk by faith, not by sight.

TAPE MEASURE

On Easter Day, a family brought Bert with them to our church. He was getting on, but not too well—just out from a spell in the hospital. I'd met him a few times over the years; he was my best mate's father-in-law. A big, genial, loving guy who would talk to anyone, ex-Para but never liked to talk about it, the kind of bloke anyone would want as a grandad. He'd never been to our church before.

In my talk that day I broached the last taboo subject in our society, the only thing you can't talk about in polite conversation: death. As a former police officer, I presented the conclusive evidence of many witnesses—that a man had claimed to be able to not only defy death but defeat it, because He was God. He proved the boast and made an offer. "There are many mansions in My Father's house; I am going to get one ready for you. Trust Me."

One of the illustrations I used was a tape measure. A very long one. I bought it for the talk and hadn't realized quite how long it was, but I held it up and said that this life that we get so wrapped up in looking after, protecting, and worrying about is just like one tiny inch on the tape measure of an eternal perspective. I got Alan, a friend on staff at the church, to grab the end of the tape measure. Then he ran way, way back to the doors of the large venue we were using. If I say so myself, it was a pretty good illustration! I said that the decisions we make in this life really do echo in eternity, and that maybe we need to live our one short life here with more of that reality in mind.

"Are you ready?" I asked. "Are you ready now, for later? Are you ready for what was here long before you got here and will always be there after you?"

I invited people to pray, or if they wanted, I or others on the team would pray for them. For healing, for themselves, to respond to the Easter message the way they felt they should.

Bert saw Alan walking past, struggled to his feet, and asked, "Please, pray like that for me."

Alan could see the man before him wasn't well. "Do you want me to pray for you to be well? For healing?"

"And the rest. All of that, everything he was saying is on offer—I want it all. All of that." They prayed, and he received it all. He got the rest.

Two days later I got a call from the family. Bert had gone home afterwards, then quite unexpectedly—he really went home, to the mansion Jesus built for him.

David asked God, "Teach us to number our days, that we may gain a heart of wisdom" (Ps. 90:12). I join him in that request. You might be successful in many ways in this mortal coil, but before you shuffle off, get wise.

DON'T JUST FIX THE BIKE, FIX THE BIKER

Back at the conference, I drilled down a little deeper with Noel and heard his story as a boy, a teen, and a man desperate to receive attention, affirmation, and unconditional positive regard from that most important of all other men. Instead, he had received rejection, indifference, and disappointment until he stopped going where he knew it wasn't to be found.

I prayed for wisdom and words; this was holy ground. As Jesus once said of another, this man was "not far from the kingdom of God" (Mark 12:34).

"What if I told you you could be adopted? Adopted by a perfect Father, who would always be available and who would delight to give you all those things?" The moment of truth.

Now all I could do was await the response and pray. You may not understand this, but for me, these moments are more exciting than bungee jumping. I was sure he could hear my heart pounding. The seconds were very long.

A gasp.

Projectile tears came from his eyes. "Yes. Oh yes, please. That's what I want, more than anything."

We prayed there and then—he entered the hairpin at speed! Last I heard, Noel was still full throttle or rather riding pillion now, holding tight behind his heavenly Father. Nothing makes me happier.

But there are far too many Noels waiting for adoption.

MY DAD'S BIGGER THAN YOUR DAD (OR MY DAD)

What about you? Ever come to the end of your ability? Good. That's where Abba comes in.

Kids with a loving dad know what to do when it's not working. They go to dad and he opens the toolbox and does what only he can do.

The Father who wants to adopt you has all kinds of tools to help you. You don't know how to make your life work? He specializes in it. He has power to open up anything that's jammed up; He can easily lift loads that would be impossible for you to carry. He can jump-start your dreams, weld together a broken marriage and make it even stronger, demolish your enemies, blow away your fears. He can straighten it, level it, build it. Just ask Dad.

Scottish poet and minister George MacDonald in *Unspoken Sermons* commented that, "The refusal to look up to God as our father is the one central wrong in the whole human affair; the inability, the one central misery."[4] He went on to explain that the word that most Bibles translate as "adoption" goes far beyond our understanding that someone who was an outsider joins a family. The word could better be translated "taken to be a son."

MacDonald says it "does not imply that God adopts children that are not his own, but rather that a second time he fathers his own; that a second time they are born—this time from above, that he will make himself tenfold, yea, infinitely their father: he will have them into the very bosom whence they issued . . . he will have them one with himself. It was for the sake of this that, in his Son, he died for them."[5]

You don't have to understand all of that to know its reality. I'll sum it up in four words personally addressed to you from the real God, the perfect Father who will take you as a son:

"Come for your hug."

Chapter 8

JESUS

"I am an historian, I am not a believer, but I must confess as a historian that this penniless preacher from Nazareth is irrevocably the very centre of history. Jesus Christ is easily the most dominant figure in all history."

– ATTRIBUTED TO H. G. WELLS

"I came to my Christian faith later in life . . . because the precepts of Jesus Christ spoke to me in terms of the kind of life that I would want to lead."

– BARACK OBAMA

"I am the resurrection and the life. The one who believes in me will live, even though they die; and whoever lives by believing in me will never die." (John 11:25–26)

– JESUS CHRIST

IT'S ALL ABOUT JESUS

AS A SPEAKER AND WRITER, I would have loved, for the sake of alliteration, to finish off this book with another "F" chapter. Maybe "Faith." But faith alone doesn't save you. It's what and who you put your faith in that matters. That's why this is all about Jesus.

TIME FOR TEA

He was in his thirties when the voice started. An inner voice, indistinct as a whisper at first, but becoming louder and more insistent:

"There's more to life."

He looked in the mirror one morning and it wasn't the love handles or the extra silver shooting through his mane that alarmed him. The years just seemed to be flying faster and he'd subtly begun to question what it was really all about.

"There is more to life."

11:10 a.m., shine right shoe by rubbing it on hallway carpet, head toward elevator.

It was a small town and he was a larger-than-life guy. Everyone knew Zac; few would call him friend. He'd made his money the hard way, through property and loans. Some called him a shark, but that's what made him a big fish. He had more than enough money now—though he could always use a little more because his earnings never could quite match his yearnings. He adjusted the diamond tiepin.

11:13 a.m., press button—satisfying ping.

Business travel and extra leisure time he'd once enjoyed now provided unwanted periods to ponder, wrestle with, and push away the nagging thoughts about what others would call success—versus significance. He had the pounds, but what about purpose? What had he ever done that really counted? Who knew him beyond the externals?

He could be funny and sharp-witted; the guys he did business with laughed along—everyone knew Zac could always be relied on to give forth with a whiskey in hand. But how many of them really despised him in secret?

He cursed as he shook off those useless thoughts. "Focus!"

Zac checked his Rolex Yacht-Master, which of course kept perfect time, but that wasn't his source of pride. It was that he himself was always punctual. Never early, never late. You could say what you wanted about Mr. Z. P. Goldstein, MBA (people said many things, some of which were untrue), but you could never say he was late.

Or early.

Just on time. On point. Exactly on time. Punctual.

Everyone knew that the elevator doors would open and he would step into the reception area at 11:14 a.m. His mother had instilled into him this value, the mark of a true gentleman. If they said, "His timing is impeccable," that said everything about a man. Timing was everything. It was something he was fastidious about. Punctuality—spelled OCD.

They could set their watches by him. The cleaners, the reception staff, the baggage clerks. He straightened starched cuffs and readied himself to go out and meet his public. The elevator doors opened and he walked through the lobby of his hotel.

His. All his. One of his hotels, one of his many business ventures.

The luxuriant carpets were his, the opulent mahogany-clad reception area, his. Onyx statues and marble busts. His.

The staff were his.

His staff. They smiled widely as they greeted him passing by, though more than once in the highly polished interiors he'd glimpsed a pale reflection of their faces changing when they thought he could not see them. He knew they complained about the wages, and he'd sacked a few old-timers, but what was a man to do in such hard economic times?

The sun momentarily scorched the top of his male-pattern baldness as he tried to cover the patch and pat it down with his embroidered handkerchief. He did not wear a yarmulke because the religion he was born into had rejected him because of his association with Gentiles and supposed collusion with the invading powers that be. He cursed again for forgetting his hat, but it shouldn't matter, except his car was now twenty seconds late! His doorman appeared Mephisto-like at his side, opening a sunshade with a flourish as he waited for the limo to appear. Now, finally, the door opened and he disappeared into the dark and cool interior.

11:15 a.m.

He'd made it.

But what have I made? "There is more to life . . ."

The driver—fat guy on Wednesdays; he could never remember their names—turned the music low to apologize and mumble some lame excuse about bad traffic as Zac received his martini. He was going to his racecourse, where he would see his horse win the 11:30. It would win because it was lighter than all the other horses. The adjudicators and officials were his. He would present the trophy himself standing with his jockey later, and the cameras would flash for the sports pages as he dripped sweat without a hat . . . but nobody would comment. At least, not out loud. Some would sneer at a distance as others cursed, screwing up their losing slips in disgust. If people didn't like him winning, they shouldn't play the game.

The blonde purring and pouring drinks in the back of the car told him how nice he looked today. She was paid well to flatter, but he received the compliment without a sound and adjusted his tie. Some said they wanted to mother him—he was more than happy to let them for a while until he got what he wanted and moved on. He was great with numbers. Why could he never remember their names?

11:17 a.m. The car stopped.

11:19 a.m. The car stayed stopped. *What's going on?*

"Sorry, sir, traffic seems snarled up. I'll try to find a way round it."

No way. Going nowhere fast, or slow. They were stuck in the middle of a vast crowd that had overflowed from the square onto the road. No one could see in through the tinted windows, but they all knew his car anyway. Some gestured rudely as the driver honked the horn louder and more insistently. He barked obscenities at nobody in particular.

11:22 a.m. "GET OUT AND SEE WHAT THE HOLDUP IS!"

"Yessir! Right away, sir!"

11:25 a.m.?! *This is intolerable in my town. Where has that driver got to? Why am I paying the clown? What's the hold up? At this rate ...*

No!

He would not permit the thought, but he couldn't push down the nauseating, dawning reality. Time waits for no man. Not even him.

At this rate, he would be ... late.

He would not pull into his private space in time. Because he was LATE.

Those assigned to clear the way through the crowd to his enclosure would pat their timepieces in disbelief. Could it be?

It could not be. The thought was intolerable.

At times, he'd been snubbed by those who considered themselves respectable because of how he'd made, not inherited, his wealth. He could live with that. Religious bigots used him in sermon illustrations as a man who had sold his soul. He could live with that. On other occasions he'd seen those whom he'd had muscled out of their (no, his!) houses spit in the street as he'd walked by. He could live with that. His own family might not like him and his wife might have left him, all calling him greedy and a liar on their way out. None of them could long live with him—but he could live with all that.

He would not, could not live with being late! He looked at the watch again and willed it to go backwards, but despite its extortionate price tag, it could not bring him the joy it promised, because he was now—officially—running late.

He made a decision. Pulled the catch back. Outside it was sweltering. The crowd was still there; in fact, it seemed to have grown. He had to push hard on the door with his shoulder to make room to step out. So was this what the worst day of Zacchaeus Goldstein's life would feel like?

There was only one thing he hated more than being late. Crowds. He hated crowds. In fact, he arranged his life to avoid crowds. On school photographs he'd always been pushed to the front, never the back row. His parents were beanstalks and said he'd grow taller soon enough, but the promised growth spurt never came. The name-calling began early. The other boys soon learned that what he lacked in size he made up for in fury when you crossed him. The girls knew not to wear heels on the red carpet with him and not get caught alongside him on camera. He preferred to walk alone.

But he always felt alone in a crowd. And small. The smallest adult, and even the kids these days were giants!

He braced himself for stares and sniggers. Was that the worst they could do? Bring it on!

A shiny size four shoe stepped out. Metal segs to give an extra inch always made a sharp clicking sound distinctly over the noise of the crowd. What noise?

No noise.

That's what was different about this crowd. Silence. A strained silence, like when everyone's trying to hear something.

"Hey! What's going on? What's the holdup? Get out of my . . ."

Hundreds of eyes looked down at him, stripped him of power with their disdain. They didn't even have to say, "Shh!"

It was silent again.

No. Not silence. There was a voice. That's what everyone was trying to hear!

Carried on the warm breeze, wafting over the tops of the infuriatingly stupid beanstalks that surrounded him. What was that voice? And what was it saying? Muffled, indistinct snatches of tantalizing promise.

"I have come, that you might have life."

Somehow familiar? He had heard that voice before somewhere. He needed to see the source. He hated this crowd more than any other. How could he make a way?

"I am the way . . . I am the truth . . . I am the life . . . If anyone comes to me, I will never turn him away."

A poet? Seriously, are all these people stopping just to listen to a poet?

"It is easier for a camel to pass through the eye of a needle . . ."

(Laughter from the crowd; is it a comedian then?)

"Than for a rich man to enter the kingdom of heaven . . ."

Is he talking about me? Who is that?

The voice didn't seem accusing; there was something joyful in every syllable. Nevertheless the crowd accused Zac as heads swiveled and eyes turned to look down at him again. Hating, accusing, jealous—but then the worst of them all? Pity.

It didn't matter that he was now late. The power in these words spoke to that other voice inside him. Seemed even to be the same voice? Nobody ever spoke like this man!

"There is more to life . . ."

What?! The voice grew louder, perhaps twenty feet away, but he couldn't see the source. Zac pushed and shoved as he pictured himself as a tiny flower being crowded out by worthless weeds. Anger started to flare, but now the voice he'd heard inside and the voice in the street spoke in tune:

"A man's life does not consist of the abundance of his possessions . . ."

No! The voice was getting quieter! He tried to push through, but the crowd closed ranks, suffocating the words. "The thief comes to steal, kill, and destroy—but I have come so you may have life in all its fullness!"

"Truly I say to you . . . unless . . . man . . .

he cannot . . .

the kingdom of God."

"What? Unless a man what?"

A red-faced man glowered at him. "Is born again. He said you have to be born again. Now shut up!"

There was only one thing to do. It didn't matter what anyone thought, he had to hear the speaker. Had to see the face behind the words that were challenging, convicting, calling. He put his hands on the hot roof, a foot in the doorway, and clambered on top of the limousine. It somehow didn't matter that the suit was creasing or the segs were scratching the roof. He pulled himself up on a nearby branch, desperate for more height. He had to hear! He had to see!

Spinning himself around, he tried to orient himself to where the voice had last come from. He looked to the front of the car and came face-to-face—with the voice.

He would tell of this first impression many times and in many other places:

This guy isn't much taller than me. Workmen's clothes. Surrounded by a gang, obviously his friends, all dressed like the guys who work at one of my factories. Ordinary? No way. Authority. He exudes it—no, it emanates from his broad smile in a way that designer clothes, jewels, and all the trappings of wealth can only promise but never really deliver. Power like a president, and something incredibly, well, good. All around him, an aura—a fragrance no perfumer could reproduce. Purity, like seeing a young bride on her wedding day.

We lock eyes and I immediately want to pull mine away, but I can't. It's like he knows me, and that cannot be good. He hasn't spoken, and for the first time in my life, it stops.

Time.

Time stops. There's a heaviness in the air that has nothing to do with the heat of the day. I want to hold my breath.

Because it's like time doesn't exist around this man, like he carries eternity around with him.

"Zacchaeus . . ."

He knows me.

He knows my name.

He knows all about me. For the first time in my life, something else happens.

I wish I weren't standing tall in a crowd.

I don't want him to notice me. I wanted to check him out from a distance. Why did I go out on a limb? Why couldn't I have stayed low in the crowd and listened to the words and let him pass? Because now everyone's looking at me, but worse than that, he's looking at me. With those eyes. Like he knows.

He knows my name. He knows it all. Every shady deal done on the side. Every bribe taken or given. Everyone I ever hurt to gain everything I own. And surely now that he knows the truth he must denounce me. He would be perfectly right to do so. It's dirty laundry time. Another voice inside accuses me, "Zacchaeus! You lying, cheating, selfish thief! Get down! You don't deserve to be here." That's what I should hear. It's what I have sometimes said to myself when lying alone at night, or when lying to someone else. The truth about me, which everyone in the crowd knows, is that I am a real, notorious sinner—and they don't even know the half of it. But then I realize that's not his voice. He's still not talking. Just smiling.

Now he opens his mouth, and smiles even more broadly, and says, "I don't have a watch. What time is it?"

I don't even have to look at mine. The internal clock says, "11:45 a.m."

"Oh, you mean tea time!" he says. "I want to come to your place!"

SHORT CHANGED

My retelling of the historical events described by Dr. Luke in his gospel (19:1–10) cannot begin to convey the sense of shock that the crowd must have felt the day a respectable, popular rabbi named Jesus of Nazareth entered a town called Jericho and bypassed the religious leaders to invite Himself to be the guest at the home of a notorious tax collector called Zacchaeus.

Jesus had already included a tax collector called Levi among His closest followers, which must have raised some eyebrows. Tax collectors were known collaborators with the hated Roman conquerors, impure because they handled their money and because they could charge as much as they wanted as long as the Romans got theirs; they of course took some of it for themselves.

Zacchaeus was a *chief* tax collector, for which we can read "universally despised."

The Jewish people place a great value on meals and hospitality. In those days, eating was much more than just eating. If I shared a meal with you, table fellowship meant I was showing you acceptance. I was saying, "I am willing to share my life with you." It was the marker of God's chosen to guard that table from the outsider and unclean. This is one reason why a Jew would not enter the home of a Gentile in those days.

If you have ever been to Sunday school this story will be familiar to you because it's an easy one for the teachers to get the kids to reenact. You always get the shortest kid to play Zacchaeus of course. That's because it says he "wanted to see who Jesus was, but because he was short he could not see over the crowd" (Luke 19:3).

One of the few interesting things I learned at theological college was that in the original Greek text it's not exactly clear who the short man of the two was. It just says Zac couldn't see Jesus because he was small. Who? Who was small? Jesus or Zacchaeus?

It could have been Zacchaeus, so I will stick with that traditional thought rather than annoy too many people. But the way my Bible tells it, Jesus of Nazareth was just as much God come among us to bring heaven to earth whether He was six-foot-four and full of muscles or a baby in a manger. When I share that thought at men's meetings, it usually elicits at least one cheer—from the little guy at the back of the room!

Some men are all about appearance, but God sees the reality. That's what Zacchaeus discovered the day Jesus cut through the camouflage of the tree he was hiding in and came to his house. I have talked about that little guy so often in men's meetings because I think he has so many lessons to teach us blokes.

Why did he climb a sycamore tree when Jesus was passing by? Perhaps it was so he could have the upper hand. He's up here—Jesus is down there. He's got God right where he wants Him. He's not anti-God, but he knows where He is if he needs Him. Lots of men I know are most comfortable keeping God at arm's length.

Jesus is having none of it.

He says, "I must stay at your house today" (Luke 19:5).

What do you do with that? Yes, I mean you.

What if He's talking to you? He knows your name.

He knows all about you. He has been talking to you too.

What would change if Jesus came to your house?

You might think you would have to tidy up first. Wrong. You might think He would come to condemn, to judge, to blame. He could. He knows you, fella. He would be totally justified, and if you disagree it's only because you're self-deceived and can add pride to the list. But that's not what He came for. Jesus came to help people find their way back to God. And the great thing is when God came to be a man, He did not become the kind of man who puts people off God! Jesus described His mission succinctly as He dabbed His lips on a fine napkin after the meal at Zacchaeus's place: "For the Son of Man came to seek and to save the lost" (v. 10).

I don't think that rich man woke up that day feeling lost, but he was. We men are not good at asking for directions, and we are certainly not going to admit to being lost, are we? From my own experience it's even worse when your wife says, "We passed the sign way back there . . ."

What do men do? We celebrate our manhood by keeping on going. Carry on regardless.

Because we want the wrong road to become the right road.

But no matter how hard you want that to happen, the wrong road just keeps getting longer and wronger. You have to change something. You have to ask for directions.

Eventually, you have to do the hardest thing for a man to do. Get off the road at a petrol station or something, turn around, and go the other way. And the Bible has a word for that. Repentance. It literally means "change your mind."

On close inspection, Zacchaeus was not living as the man God made him to be. His flaws are all too apparent. The great news in the story is that Jesus knew all that and still accepted him. He loved him as he was. Jesus went home with him, insisted on it—even though Zacchaeus wasn't religious or even a very good person (both of which actually make having Jesus at home very hard indeed).

Everyone in town said, "Why has Jesus gone to be the guest of a notorious sinner?" But Zacchaeus wasn't listening to the crowd. He opened his home, and his heart, and the friendship developed.

It seems the chief tax collector really did recognize that he was accepted in truly exalted company as he said, "Look, Lord! Here and now I give half of my possessions to the poor, and if I have cheated anybody out of anything, I will pay back four times the amount" (v. 8). (If?!)

I don't think Jesus told him to do that. This was the start of a process of a man being formed for and living out the true potential he was made for: a man with nothing to prove and nothing to hide. A man who could be tough, transparent, trusted. Because now, he knew he was treasured!

Jesus didn't come to his house to pore over the accounts, but to pour the teapot (they were both Englishmen of course!). There was something about being befriended, loved, and welcomed by the Son of God that made all that other stuff seem so much less valuable in comparison. He was changed from the inside out.

Then, Zac went to work on his *finances*. We had a chapter about that, didn't we? Who knows, maybe the next thing was his *fitness* and he signed up for the Jericho 10k? Perhaps he got back in touch with some of his *family* to apologize and attempt to rebuild those relationships? Knowing God as his *Father*, having Jesus as his best *friend* and seeing how close He was with His disciples, wouldn't he want to learn how to be a better friend now? I don't know what happened next, but I know the change happens not from us trying harder (been there, not done that). This is not a self-help book; self-help leaves you helpless and selfish. We might try to change the outside, but the way God works is from the inside out.

INSIDE JOB

Centuries before Jesus walked into that town, another man that others thought too small to take on giant tasks had a surprising God encounter. A prophet called Samuel came to a little town called

Bethlehem (before it or any of its inhabitants were famous) to select the new king of Israel from among the sons of a man called Jesse (1 Sam. 16:1–13).

I picture them lined up in height order. Any man who was never picked for the football team knows what it is to be in that line. The youngest boy, whom the siblings are jealous of and the father is dismissive of, isn't even at the party. He's away doing a servant's job, looking after the sheep. Samuel looks and thinks the oldest son looks the part. But God rejects them all one by one:

> *Do not look on his appearance or on the height of his stature, because I have rejected him. For the LORD sees not as man sees: man looks on the outward appearance, but the LORD looks on the heart.*
> 1 Samuel 16:7 (ESV)

This is a word for us, men. "The LORD sees not as man sees." Do you see that yet? God saw what David's own earthly father never saw—He saw the man David was made to be. How does He see you? How do you see yourself?

UP CLOSE AND PERSONAL

Well done for reading this far. Most men don't read anything except the paper or anything they are made to read for work—I commend and thank you. There are fewer pages at this end of the book, and I hope decision time approaches for some of you, not only about the external changes you might want to make on the outside but also about the inside that matters to God.

I want to start to get close and personal as Jesus did with the little coal man of Jericho now. What's your next step after reading the book? I hope, if nothing else, what I've written will give you an appetite to go and get a Bible. I encourage people to start with Mark's gospel; it's the shortest—you can read it all in about the time you would read a daily paper. Rather than rely on what anyone else might have told you about that most amazing of all books, actually read it for yourself. I find if I start my morning reading a portion of the Bible, the story of that day always goes better.

Check out the eyewitness accounts I've only had a chance to allude to. They are not just inspiring, they are inspired. Maybe you can imagine yourself in the story as these historical events took place, observing the action (that's what I did to write the story at the start of this chapter). This invitation comes with a spiritual health warning, however: be prepared for Jesus Christ to walk off the pages and show you that He knows you too, as He's done for countless millions before you.

IT HAPPENED TO ME

At junior school I was told the stories of Jesus; I probably heard Zacchaeus's story in some assembly or religious study class. Perhaps it was even mentioned in the obligatory hours in chapel, which convinced me there was a purgatory—sitting through the services. I heard that Jesus was the Son of God, that He had died for the sins of the world. It meant little to me.

When I was thirteen I decided to "give God a go"—to see if He was there, hoping He wasn't so I could get on with life without Him, with myself fully in charge. I got the early bus and endured services almost every day in Lent, and though there were various liturgical prayers being intoned, I said only one: "If there's anybody up there you'd better show me you're real. Show me—or I'm out of here."

Nothing. I looked at the statue of Jesus hanging on a cross. It didn't cry. No sound from heaven. No sign of God.

Good. If there was no God I could live however I wanted (I'd figured out the natural consequences of atheism pretty early on), treat people as I wanted. I was just another causeless animal adrift on an aimless planet. I just wanted some action out of life before I died and ceased to exist like everything else.

As high school drew to a close, I visited the careers advisor and told her I wanted to join either the army or the police. She asked what my parents did. "They work in a cotton mill."

"You should work in the mill."

"I don't want to work in the mill."

"What does your older brother do?" she asked.

"He works in the same mill." (Terry's summer job there has now lasted over thirty years.)

"You should work in the mill."

"I don't want to work in the mill."

"What's wrong with working in the mill?"

"Nothing, I just want to join the police."

"No chance—you're too small!"

"I'm sixteen. I think I might grow. Anyway I've heard they have Police Cadets; I wonder if you have any information on that?"

"No, but I can help you apply if you want to work in the mill."

At sixteen I told my parents I was going to college. I went out one morning, got there late, played table tennis, and then went to my Italian friend and boxing training partner Pete's house to drink his dad's homemade wine all afternoon. Then I went home and tried to seem sober. That lasted about a month with nobody knowing except Pete and me. I think Pete's dad started to guess though because he began to hide the *vino tinto*. I decided I really had to get a job or my dad would kill me, so I applied for the Police Cadets.

I went for the test for the police and passed the written intelligence examinations. There were medicals too. Having done the eyesight test, the optician said, "You have sniper vision." I was downcast. You mean some stupid problem with my eyes was going to keep me out of the police? He explained that it wasn't a bad thing but a good thing, then asked if I'd taken the intelligence test yet.

A few days later I went for the interview for the Police Cadets. There was a panel of three, but a dour Scottish inspector was the only one who spoke. "It says on your CV you like doing magic card tricks." I did then; it was an interest, the kind of thing your mum says is a waste of time because you'll never get a job doing that.

He opened a drawer in the desk. "Amaze me."

I did a fairly rubbish trick and got the job. Mum's not always right.

I bumped into the careers woman a week later. She was delighted. "I've never got anyone into the Police Cadets before!"

The Cadets bore little relation to real police work it turned out, but it was brilliant in its own way. In two years I put on tons of muscle and got super fit, learning judo and aikido. I also discovered canoeing, climbing, and carnal knowledge.

One quiet evening on security duty, while I was walking around the Training College, I saw a poster on the wall that some religious nutter had put up: "Christian Police Association Meeting, Thursday, 7pm." Some voice inside that sounded like my own said, "You should go to that."

"Nah! No way!" I carried on. But even now I could take you to that exact spot where the poster was.

Jesus is the ultimate "fisher of men," and it was like God had a hook in my heart. But I pulled away on the line and wasn't going to come easily.

At eighteen and a half years of age I was a police officer walking nights in Cheetham Hill, one of the toughest beats in the UK. The officer who showed me the ropes also showed me that although I'd thought I could drink, I was way behind him. The depiction in the BBC TV drama *Life on Mars* was close, but somewhat understated.

The force was unbelievable in terms of drinking, womanizing, and violence. I lived for all three. Finally, life had purpose.

The miners' strike erupted, and I became one of the bad guys in *Billy Elliot*. Scary, hairy times, the closest thing to civil war the nation has gone through in living memory. I was at what became known as the Battle of Orgreave, on the day that Arthur Scargill was arrested. Mum had told me to keep my head down. I was two rows back from the front line. I thought I was safe, until the coke trucks driven by working miners came into view. Suddenly, thousands of huge, angry miners were pushing thousands of their "enemy" policemen, and the force of the two buckled against one another. I found myself pushed up on the crest of a human wave, unable to breathe or move at all. I became an Aunt Sally as delighted miners began to throw bricks and sticks at my pale head.

I think after the miners' strike I lost it for a few years. I don't want to go into too much detail, and I'm not proud of this. There are some things I did I don't even want to try to remember, but I was definitely in slow self-destruct mode.

I hurt some good people. Too many women, some of whom were happy to just have sex but some who wanted a relationship I was neither interested in nor capable of. I also enjoyed hurting bad people. I found I was quite good at violence as I got bigger, and working where I did gave me good opportunity to learn how to get better at it.

One day I turned a corner to see a lad my age trying to nick a car. I chased him awhile until he suddenly stopped running. He figured he could take me in a fight and we had a long time finding out. Only at the station did I discover he was one of the infamous Noonan brothers who went on to achieve legendary status as Manchester's gangster baddies.

The drinking was getting worse and worse. I had my own apartment at twenty, a place where I was utterly unaccountable to anyone.

I sometimes went to work as a police officer with a mouthful of extra strong mints to hide the smell of drink.

I was badly beaten up by a gang one night as I came out of a nightclub alone. A football hooligan I was at school with pointed me out as an off-duty copper, and I found myself surrounded, nose broken and on the floor for a good kicking. It was the worst beating of my life, but we did manage to bring most of them to justice later. I discovered the hard way that night that I was not invincible, but I applied for the riot squad because I was determined that I would from then on always be on the winning side.

Around that time a nurse called Zoe heard about this wild and out-of-control policeman. She was engaged to a fireman I knew. 999. When she first saw me she didn't like what she saw. I still remember seeing her and thinking, "Tasty, but too posh."

New Year's Eve, some nightclub. I'd had more than a few but had developed a high tolerance. I saw a lovely girl dancing. As midnight struck, I put myself in front of her for a kiss and it happened. A great kiss—one of the three greatest in history—spoiled only by her fiancé (the fireman) who pushed me from behind and took a swing at me. Within minutes we were both thrown out by the bouncers. I know it's not your usual "how the church minister met his wife" story.

A few weeks later Zoe broke up their relationship. Nothing to do with me—she had made a commitment to follow Jesus Christ a few years before and realized that her life wasn't lining up with that. It was him or God, so he went.

I tried to move in. No way. She only wanted a friend.

I'll be your friend.

Eventually I got her to go to the pictures with me "as a friend." Great film. A classic rom-com. Arnold Schwarzenegger in *Commando*. She didn't like it for some reason. Good thing it was cheap night. But there was something different about this one. Something shone from her—a diamond girl—but I was a coal man through and through. She said we could be friends but that she wouldn't be interested in any further relationship because I wasn't a Christian. I told her actually I was because it's a Christian country. "No," she said, "the Hindus and Muslims would disagree."

Her ex approached me in a pub. "You better finish with Zoe—she's a weirdo. She's one of these 'born again' Christians."

I knew it was sour grapes. "No she's not; she's not an American."

I tried to put her off God anyway and get her more into me. I asked all those tough questions, like, "How did Noah get all those animals on the ark?" and "What did they do for forty days and forty nights?"

"I suppose they went fishing."

"They couldn't do much with only two worms."

I told her about some of the terrible things I'd seen: "A young girl last week stabbed her mum to death, to save her sisters because the mum was going to set them all on fire. How can there be a good God when that happens?" I wasn't interested in the answer, just knew it was a good one to get God-botherers squirming.

She didn't try to convert me, which was infuriating. "I know what I believe. What you believe is up to you."

One day she said, "You keep asking these questions. If you really want to know what I believe there's a man coming and speaking at a church next week. I have to be at that to help with the kids' work. If you want you can come."

That sounded like a date!

"Only if I can take you to the pub after?" I'd even put up with a bit of church for that.

"Okay."

I went into the church building and was amazed to see it full. Full of smiling people who actually looked normal and like they wanted to be there. The music was actually good too—in church!

Then there was a drama—in church!

Acted by young people—in church!

I only remember the end. A guy in a white T-shirt, who I figured was Jesus, saying he was the light of the world. But then he was dragged up a stepladder and they stretched out his arms wide and mimed hammering nails in as someone read some words, which I later found came straight from the Bible:

This is the verdict: Light has come into the world, but people loved darkness instead of light because their deeds were evil. Everyone who does evil hates the light, and will not come into the light for fear that their deeds will be exposed.
John 3:19, 20

Well, that was me. But I wasn't about to admit it. If you'd asked, I considered myself to be a very good person. You could probably have found any number of ex-girlfriends and criminals who'd disagree, but after all I was a police officer, ready for inspection with shiny buttons on my uniform, shiny teeth, shiny boots. If I ever felt bad about my own track record, I could always arrest another baddy to compare myself with so I would feel better.

After the drama, a man got up to speak. Oh good. He would be boring and irrelevant. Wrong again. Eric Delve is one of the finest, most passionate, and most gifted orators the church in England has ever produced. He produced a nail, held it aloft: "This is the kind of nail Jesus would have had driven into Him . . ." With fire in his eyes he described how the cross was not just a story but history. Not an item of jewelry but an instrument of torturous execution. Calvary was not an example of what happens when a good man gets a raw deal but was where the Son of God was whipped, stripped, beaten beyond recognition, and abandoned by those closest to Him.

He graphically described how on that darkest day Jesus Christ bore our sins, became our sins. Jesus the holy Son of God became the sin of Adam, of every man who had ever lived and broken the laws of God. The only innocent bore the punishment so guilty ones could be acquitted. Jesus predicted in detail that He would die as a ransom for many—and rise again from the dead to prove His claims, and then He did!

"Well, that was pretty good, Zoe. Good speaker. Let's get to the pub."

A few evenings later I went to the meeting again, in the same condition. There is a verse in the Bible that says it's possible for people to make their hearts "as hard as a diamond" so they can't hear what God is saying (Zech. 7:12 NASB). That was me.

At the end they offered some free literature if anyone was interested. Well, I found it interesting—did that count? I decided I might try church one Sunday. I went to the front as the band played something majestic and got my free books. Zoe's mum hugged me and seemed very excited, but I took the books home unread and put them in the sock drawer.

CRACKING THE CODE

A few days later Zoe had a present for me. Things were definitely looking up. I opened it. But it was a Bible. That was very weird, but I said I liked it. I told her I was definitely a Christian. She didn't buy it.

Then I opened it. She'd written inside:

To Anthony
    Mark 8:34
    Love Zoe

"Love!"
She put "love" there! Get in!
The stuff in the middle must be a code. The ex was called Mark.

Was this about him? Saying I'm better than him? No. It must be in the Bible, stupid. She helped me find the gospel of Mark. I was thinking this verse might say, "Okay, because I think you are good looking and funny, I will go out with you." It didn't say that. That's nowhere in the Bible, I've since discovered.

It said, "Then he called the crowd to him along with his disciples and said: 'Whoever wants to be my disciple must deny themselves and take up their cross and follow me.'"

What cross? Jesus had a cross. Who else needed a cross? "I don't know what this means."

"The fact that you don't know what it means, means you're not a Christian."

Poo.

I really liked this girl! I decided to go to church with her a bit; maybe that would fool her.

A few weeks later, I was driving to work in a Mini (the car, not a skirt; I wasn't undercover or anything). Someone from her church had lent me a tape with some of the more modern kind of songs they were using, so I put it on. It was just background music on the road through a hard part of the city called Gorton. One song came on called "The Servant King."

Hands that flung stars into space
To cruel nails surrendered[1]

What was that? Wind it back. (You could do that with tapes! Who says technology has moved on?)

Hands that flung stars into space
To cruel nails surrendered

Wham. What follows next might freak you out. It did me. For good. Forever.

The presence of God invaded the car. That is the only way I can describe it. Somehow, I pulled over to the side of the road, as I had a full-on, technicolor, 3D vision of Jesus Christ on the cross. Blood—and guts. Such courage. I knew that Jesus was the toughest man who ever lived, because of what I saw Him endure in that vision. I also knew He is the Son of God, because He was alive, and He was coming closer to me.

Oh no!

He is God.

He knows. About me.

He knows it all. What nobody else knows. What nobody should ever know.

He has seen it all, heard it all, as I did it all. He is the truth and He knows the truth.

I felt like I was covered in excrement as this indescribable purity of holiness drew closer. I didn't even know the Ten Commandments, but I knew I must have broken them all. I wanted to die. I deserved to die. I wanted to hide, but it's hard to hide from God in a Mini.

I had been in court many times as a witness. There is an authority about such places. I loved to see the guilty punished. But what about me? Magnify the awe of a human courtroom immeasurably as I began to despair at the thought that Jesus is God and He could and should—He must—judge me. I deserved any sentence He would pronounce. Just then . . .

Grace.

Love.

Mercy. So sweet and undeserved.

Grace, grace, grace upon grace.

"You are My son. I have always loved you. I love you, Son. I forgive you. You didn't know. I have a plan for you. Grace. Follow

Me. Mercy. Grace. Love. Love. Let Me in. Grace."

I knew from being a boy that "Jesus died for the sins of the whole world." I just didn't know that meant me.

"Let Me take over your life. Give it to Me."

Now, it was personal. He had done everything for me.

"Yes, Lord." That was all it took and all I wanted to say. I said it. I said yes.

I never saw the Jesus statue cry, but now my tears were flowing. I hadn't cried since being a little boy—except when I watched *Shenandoah*, and that's between me and you. You'd have had to hit me very hard to make me cry. God didn't even lay a finger on me. But I cried, all right. I have no idea how long this lasted but then I was late for work.

The sergeant asked why: "I'm a Christian, Sarge."

"Well, you're not a very good one. You're late!"

I rang Zoe and told her. She believed me. She believed it had really happened to me. I knew what Mark 8:34 meant. I had cracked the code.

THE ADVENTURE

Since then, I have never had a boring day. I've had a few tedious minutes and a lot of mundane hours, I'll grant you—but from the day I yielded myself to follow God's plan for my life right up to now, it has been an adventure. If that is not your experience of following Him, you are not as close as He wants you to be. I stayed in the police for another eight years and loved serving God there. During that time He called me to really know my Bible and then train so He could use me to tell more people about Him—a long story for another time. He has transformed me from someone afraid to even speak a prayer out loud in a room of ten people to someone who has been privileged to speak to thousands and (on the radio) even millions.

Following God's plan was far better, bigger, and bolder than any I could have dreamed up for myself, and the best is yet to come. The openings to travel, speak, and tell others about Him in the nations are unbelievable for a lad from an inner-city council estate.

I have only ever loved one woman and I'm committed to faithfully enjoying loving her for the rest of my life. My children love and serve God, and now there are grandchildren, which is mind-blowing. I have witnessed miracles of healing, provision, and life change. God has taken me with Him around the world as His mouthpiece and to disaster zones, including India after the Boxing Day tsunami and Haiti right after the 2010 earthquake, to be His hands and feet to help others. Now He has brought me back to the city I grew up in to be part of His work here again with a great church family and to start a network of thousands of new reproducing churches helping people find their way back to God. I loved serving the law, but it's so much better sharing grace.

It's my conviction, looking back, that God was always watching over my life. He protected me so many times and I came away crediting myself with good luck. He was speaking to me well before that climactic moment of decision. He was more obviously there when I stood at that poster, and less so in church as a child, but He was always there. Always faithful, always loving, always calling, always my Father. Many biblical characters came to the same staggering conclusion. King David looked back over a remarkable life and traced the hand of God even back to the time when "you created my inmost being; you knit me together in my mother's womb.... Your eyes saw my unformed body; all the days ordained for me were written in your book before one of them came to be" (Ps. 139:13, 16).

I read what the apostle Paul wrote two thousand years ago to an early group of Christ followers in a place called Ephesus and found that the three-act drama of God's work in their lives mirrors my own exactly: you could label it BC, JC, AD—or even *Wow, How, Now*.

WOW

As for you, you were dead *in your transgressions and sins, in which you used to live."*
Ephesians 2:1, 2 (emphasis added)

Until I met Jesus, I wasn't bad and needing to get better; I was dead in sin and needing resurrection. Wow! I had no power to help or change myself in any real and lasting ways. I needed divine, outside intervention to accomplish internal transformation. I could not save myself; I couldn't help myself. That's the bad news. You need to know how bad the bad news is before you will gladly welcome the good news.

HOW

It is by grace you have been saved, through faith—and this is not from yourselves, it is the gift of God—not by works, so that no one can boast.
Ephesians 2:8–9

As part of basic training in the police, I had to become qualified as a lifeguard. One of the first things you learn is that you can't save someone who's trying to save themselves. For the first twenty-one years of my life, God's grace was on offer, but it was a gift I didn't think I needed any more than a flower offered by a Hare Krishna at the airport. When I was ready and stopped trying to be good enough, He showed me that His love is great enough. What Jesus had done by suffering for sin in my place already made me acceptable. I was invited not to work for my salvation but *work out* its implications in my life.

NOW

For we are God's handiwork, created in Christ Jesus to do good works, which God prepared in advance for us to do.
Ephesians 2:10

Too often Christians stop at the previous stage. Ask forgiveness from Jesus as fire insurance, a "get out of hell free" card, then pretty much live for themselves and depend on themselves. But following Jesus is not a life change, it's a life exchange. God's grace is far more than what God gives us one day so He doesn't have to punish us for our sins. It's what fuels a new life. I heard the late James Ryle describe grace as "the empowering presence of God, enabling me to be all God calls me to be and do all God calls me to do." If you receive amazing grace every day, you will live an amazing life.

You are your heavenly Father's workmanship; His favorite project is to form you into the man you were made to be. Now He put this book into your hands as part of His purpose to help you look, think, and act like His Son, to become like His Son. He has laid out before you now a destiny, a great purpose, a difference to make today—and His grace enables it to become a reality.

MAN IN THE MIRROR

A man checks in at a run-down hotel and is asked, "Do you have a good memory for faces?"

"Yes I do."

"Good. You'll need it when you shave because there's no mirror in your room."

Did you know Jesus had younger brothers and sisters? How hard would that have been? How many times do you think they were told off with, "Why can't you be like your older brother?"

The siblings didn't believe that Jesus really was the Son of God—familiarity breeds contempt. One of the brothers was called James, and he didn't believe right up until after he saw Jesus die on the cross. He was only transformed when Jesus, his half-brother, burst open the tombstone and reappeared alive again before him.

Actually, a case could be made that none of the disciples were fully convinced followers of Jesus as the Son of God until after the resurrection. They were followers of Jesus the remarkable but human rabbi of Nazareth, trying to pattern their lives around His teaching and example. It's possible to do that, to have Jesus as your life coach and have many of the principles of wisdom work in your life, but that's not why He came, because that's not all He is.

Bono sums it up:

> Christ took on the sins of the world, so that what we put out did not come back to us [. . .] our sinful nature does not reap the obvious death. That's the point. It should keep us humbled . . . It's not our good works that get us through the gates of Heaven. [. . .]
>
> [. . .] the secular response to the Christ story always goes like this: he was a great prophet, obviously an interesting guy, had a lot to say along the lines of other prophets. [. . .] But actually Christ doesn't allow you that. [. . .] Christ says: *No. I'm not saying I'm a teacher, don't call me teacher. I'm not saying I'm a prophet. I'm saying: "I'm the Messiah."* [. . .] And people say, *No, no, please, just be a prophet. A prophet, we can take.*[2]

Within a few decades of becoming a fully convinced follower of Jesus Christ, James wrote a very practical instructional note to other believers, and he says the teaching of the Bible is like a mirror:

Act on what you hear! Those who hear and don't act are like those who glance in the mirror, walk away, and two minutes later have no idea who they are, what they look like.
James 1:22–24 (MSG)

He said it's possible to be deceived, even to deceive ourselves. You can come to the end of a book like this or even read the whole Bible and think that is what counts. Don't kid yourself—reading the highway code doesn't make you a driver. Unless you do something, it's useless. What do you do?

Explore the concepts. Go back through the book. Did you highlight like I said? What jumped out at you? What made you think in each of the different sections?

Examine yourself, your current reality. If you were pushed in one of these diamond facets—finances, family, father, friendships, etc.—which one would you crumble in? Where do you shine?

Establish a plan. What changes do you need to make? Many of the principles outlined will work for anyone and help you live a fuller life, whether you believe in Jesus Christ or not. But it would be a tragedy if you got fitter physically and lived a few years longer but didn't get ready for eternity or grow spiritually, or worked on your finances at the cost of your soul.

Engage in community with others, go and check out a good church—it may take a while, there are some terrible ones—and seek to apply what you're being shown. Maybe you're not ready yet to become a Christ follower, but even if you believe that a fraction of what I have said is true, you're at the brink of making the most important decision of your life.

THE PERFECT MAN

What I've tried to do in my own imperfect way is hold up a man to you, a perfect, absolutely flawless man. The only perfect man.

Have you seen yourself in the mirror? Do you have an accurate picture?

Are you getting the true picture of who Jesus Christ really is?

That false, stained-glass portrayal of a pale, thin, bearded man in a nightie with a shiny plate around His head has surely put off enough men by now. I don't think Jesus ever looked like that; I never met a builder who did—and I know for a fact that He doesn't look like that now, because I've read the end of the story—the book of Revelation. When the real Jesus showed up at the end of the Bible to a man who had known Him as a friend, the awesome power He radiated caused John to fall to the ground like a dead man.

The real Jesus depicted is not "gentle Jesus, meek and mild" (He's been there and done that). He is an unbeatable warrior! His face shines brighter than the noonday sun. He is resplendent in majesty, all-powerful, arms like rods of chrysolite. He is known as Faithful and True; He holds a sword, and He goes to battle with a robe dipped in the blood of His enemies as He fights for justice and wages war against evil.

He wants you to join the fight alongside Him, and this is a good fight because the victory is already complete and assured, because the name tattooed on His leg tells us who He is: "KING OF KINGS AND LORD OF LORDS" (Rev. 19:16).

This Jesus, the man from heaven, wants to come to your home. The Bible says that His dwelling place is with men, to live in your heart by faith while He gets you ready to reign with Him in eternity. I tell children Jesus wants to live in their hearts and they accept that in a simple way. Adults struggle with the physics of it. That's why He said we must be childlike in our faith if we're ever going to see the kingdom of God.

I'm asking you now, before you close the book, to do willingly in advance what you will do one day anyway. Submit your life to His leadership. He is Lord. Simply believe, trust, and declare the indisputable truth about Jesus while it has power to save you rather than condemn you. Jesus Christ is Lord! Tell Him you will live to serve Him. Offer back to Him all your time, treasure, and talents, and get ready for your adventure to unfold.

There will come a day when all creation will see Him as He is now and acknowledge the truth about Him. You will see Him too, either when you die or at His return. The Bible doesn't warn us of that to scare us but to prepare us! Everyone will see Him, even those who pierced Him. There will be no denying His greatness and glory then. Those who have denied or blasphemed Him will bend a knee and will have to speak the truth about the only perfect man.

You, me, and everyone who ever lived will one day kneel in the dust from which we were made. He will separate the people into sheep and goats, lost and found. All people will be gathered in like a great net full of fish and then the sorting will be quick and accurate.

People from every nation will be there. All mouths will acknowledge Him—even those who never spoke in this life, shouting loud alongside the humble saint who suffered and was martyred for that truth, bowing down to declare it gladly. So too the devils, doubters, and deniers will acknowledge what evil always wants to suppress. The Truth will come out—self-evident to the whole of creation.

Nearly thirty years ago I first saw this Jesus as He really is, as He is now, and everything changed for me. Forever. You may not have any kind of vision like me. God had to show Himself to me in that way because I was so hard and so far from Him. But you have your own life and He has His own way to reach you, and this book is part of that. Don't miss it. You do not need that kind of experience for Christ to change your life and your eternal destiny. Recognize and admit today that Jesus' life, death, and resurrection prove who He really is. Lord of all. Then invite Him to be Lord of you.

If you are ready to make that step, you could choose to use the next few words as a prayer, or simply use your own words. God can see your heart and hear your thoughts.

As you are sitting reading this book now, you can say something like this to God:

"Father God, I don't want to be a coal man any longer. You see the man I was made to be; shape me now. Do what You have to do in me to do what You need to do through me. I want to be adopted into Your family. I have looked in the mirror of Your perfection and I know I'm not the man I should be. Jesus, I need Your forgiveness, grace, and power to be who only You can make me. In how I look after myself and what You give me, in my friendships, family, in my failures—in every facet I invite the Holy Spirit of God to shape me and change me—from the inside out. Thank You for accepting me and coming to my house. Be Lord of my life today and always."

It will happen: you will become a new man, a new creation. The old has gone, the new has come. Christ in YOU is the hope of glory!

Because His blood stained a cross
One day every knee will bow
He was silent as a sheep before the shearers
So every tongue will confess

Because He was flogged, rejected, abandoned, and mocked
Every knee will bow
He did not use His power for His own salvation—but ours
Every tongue will confess

Because His death paid a debt He did not owe,
that we could never pay
Every knee! Your knee!
He wore a crown of thorns, now many crowns,
tasted death then spat it out
Every tongue! Yours and mine!

Because the eyes closed in death now blaze with living fire
My knee bows
Crushed for my iniquities, wounded for my transgressions, stripped for
my healing
My tongue confesses that
Jesus Christ is Lord!

Because He cried out, "It is finished!"
when I see Him, I will know Him,
because I will be like Him—God's precious
Diamond.

Notes

Chapter 1: Show Us What You're Made Of

1. Örjan Falk et al., "The 1 % of the Population Accountable for 63 % of All Violent Crime Convictions," *Social Psychiatry and Psychiatric Epidemiology* 49, no. 4 (2014): 560, https://doi.org/10.1007/s00127-013-0783-y.

2. E. Ann Carson, "Prisoners in 2018," U.S. Department of Justice, April 2020, https://bjs.ojp.gov/content/pub/pdf/p18.pdf, 3.

3. Funke Baffour, "Male Suicide: A Silent Epidemic," British Psychological Society, April 9, 2018, https://www.bps.org.uk/blogs/dr-funke-baffour/male-suicide-silent-epidemic; "Suicides in England and Wales: 2020 Registrations," Office for National Statistics, September 7, 2021, https://www.ons.gov.uk/peoplepopulationandcommunity/birthsdeathsandmarriages/deaths/bulletins/suicidesintheunitedkingdom/2020registrations.

4. David Murrow, *Why Men Hate Going to Church*, completely revised and updated (Nashville: Thomas Nelson, 2011), 60.

5. C. H. Spurgeon, *A Good Start: A Book for Young Men and Women*, 1898, p. 16, quoted in Norman Vance, *The Sinews of the Spirit: The Ideal of Christian Manliness in Victorian Literature and Religious Thought* (Cambridge: Cambridge University Press, 1985), 26.

Chapter 2: Fitness

1. William McCoy, "What Is a Normal Heart Rate for Men?," Livestrong.com, https://www.livestrong.com/article/152337-what-is-a-normal-heart-rate-for-men/.

2. "The Annual Hims 2021 Men's Health Survey," ForHims.com, medically reviewed by Kristin Hall, last updated May 27, 2021, https://www.forhims.com/blog/2021-mens-health-survey.

3. https://www.gov.uk/government/publications/health-matters-getting-every-adult-active-every-day/health-matters-getting-every-adult-active-every-day.

4. https://digital.nhs.uk/data-and-information/publications/statistical/statistics-on-obesity-physical-activity-and-diet/statistics-on-obesity-physical-activity-and-diet-england-2019/part-3-adult-obesity. In the USA the figure is even higher at 73.7% https://www.niddk.nih.gov/health-information/health-statistics/overweight-obesity.

5. "Benefits of Exercise," NHS, https://www.nhs.uk/live-well/exercise/exercise-health-benefits/.

Chapter 3: Finances

1. "United Kingdom Public Sector Net Debt to GDP," https://tradingeconomics.com/united-kingdom/government-debt-to-gdp.

2. Lucy Gordon, "New Research from Savoo.co.uk Shows Work Pressures are Causing Fathers to Become Detached from Family Life," PRWeb, June 19, 2010, https://www.prweb.com/releases/2010/06/prweb4163514.htm.

3. Jane Denton, "How a British Household Spends £1.9m over a Lifetime—and the Average 50-Year-Old Has Already Spent £1m," This is Money, February 9, 2017, updated February 10, 2017, https://www.thisismoney.co.uk/money/bills/article-4208526/UK-households-spend-1-9m-lifetime.html.

4. Attributed to John Bright in *Book of Facts* (Pleasantville, NY: Reader's Digest Association, 1995), 80. However, this quotation has also been attributed to other people. See https://quoteinvestigator.com/2014/06/10/self-made/ for more information about the attribution.

5. Edmund Burke, *A Vindication of Natural Society*, 1756, https://www.gutenberg.org/files/15043/15043-h/15043-h.htm#A_VINDICATION_OF_NATURAL_SOCIETY.

6. *The Collected Works of Mahatma Gandhi*, Volume XII, April 1913 to December 1914, Gandhi Heritage Portal, https://www.gandhiheritageportal.org/cwmg_volume_thumbview/MTI=#page/1/mode/2up.

7. Andrew Fennell, "What Is the Average UK Salary?," StandOut CV, updated November 2021, https://standout-cv.com/pages/average-uk-salary.

8. Andrea Peer, "Global Poverty: Facts, FAQs, and How to Help," World Vision, updated on August 23, 2021, https://www.worldvision.org/sponsorship-news-stories/global-poverty-facts.

9. "What Percentage of Income Does the Average American Give to Charity?," AskingTheLot.com, https://askingthelot.com/what-percentage-of-income-does-the-average-american-give-to-charity/.

10. Lydia Catling, "Britons Are Throwing Away £2,675 in Rotten Food Every Year Because They Don't Know It Needs to Go in the Fridge, Research Reveals," *Daily*

Mail, December 25, 2020, https://www.dailymail.co.uk/news/article-9083719/
Food-waste-UK-Brits-throw-away-42-food-buy-cut-down.html.

11. "World Child Hunger Facts," WorldHunger.org, https://www.worldhunger.org/
world-child-hunger-facts/.

Chapter 4: Family

1. Marcus Buckingham, *One Thing You Need to Know: . . . About Great Managing,
Great Leading, and Sustained Individual Success* (New York: Free Press, 2005), 22.
Bold in original.

Chapter 5: Failure

1. Quoted in Rick Ezell, "Sermon: Run the Race - Hebrews 12," Lifeway, January 1, 2014,
https://www.lifeway.com/en/articles/sermon-run-the-race-faith-hebrews-12.

2. Theodore Roosevelt, "Citizenship in a Republic," Theodore Roosevelt Center,
Paris, France, April 23, 1910, https://www.theodorerooseveltcenter.org/Learn-
About-TR/TR-Encyclopedia/Culture-and-Society/Man-in-the-Arena.aspx.

Chapter 6: Friends

1. Deborah Tannen, *You Just Don't Understand: Women and Men in Conversation*
(New York: Ballantine Books, 1990), 128.

2. R. A. Hill and R. I. M Dunbar, "Social Network Size in Humans," *Human Nature*
14, no. 1 (2003): 53–72, https://doi.org/10.1007/s12110-003-1016-y.

3. Walt Mason, *The Sentinel*, January 1923, 16.

4. "2010 Haiti Earthquake Facts and Figures," Disasters Emergency Committee,
https://www.dec.org.uk/article/2010-haiti-earthquake-facts-and-figures.

Chapter 7: Father

1. A. W. Tozer, *The Knowledge of the Holy* (San Francisco: HarperSanFrancisco,
1961), 1.

2. Gordon Dalbey, "Father Hunger," abbafather.com, https://www.abbafather.com/
articles/article_fh.pdf.

3. Jim Shaffer, "The Prodigal or Where Am I in the Story?," *The "Second" Look*
(blog), February 28, 2013, https://jshaffer1954.wordpress.com/2013/02/28/
the-prodigal-or-where-am-i-in-the-story/.

4. George MacDonald, *Unspoken Sermons, Series I., II., and III.*, https://www
.gutenberg.org/cache/epub/9057/pg9057.html.

5. Ibid.

Chapter 8: Jesus

1. Graham Kendrick, "The Servant King," copyright © 1983 Thankyou Music.

2. *Bono: In Conversation with Michka Assayas* (New York: Riverhead, 2005), 204. Bracketed ellipses indicate omissions.

If you're imperfect... and your spouse is imperfect...
then is a healthy, vibrant marriage possible?

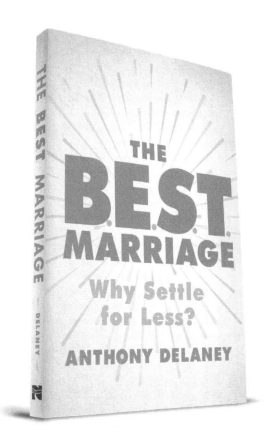

Don't trust your instincts—there is a better
path to becoming a better man.

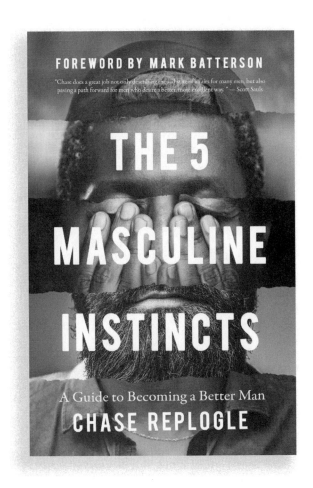

By examining the lives of five men of the Bible, *The 5
Masculine Instincts* shows that your own instincts are
neither curse nor virtue. Through exploring sarcasm,
adventure, ambition, reputation, and apathy, you'll
come to understand yourself and how your instincts
can be matured into something better.

978-0-8024-2554-6 | also available as an eBook

We were created to work, and feel most
happy, alive, and useful doing the work
we were created to do.

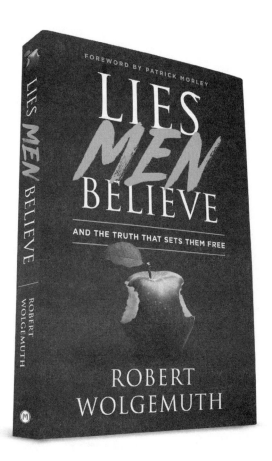